8 SUCCESSFUL BUSINESS WOMEN

8 SUCCESSFUL BUSINESS WOMEN

Prerna Kaul Mishra

Vitasta

Vitasta Publishing Pvt. Ltd.
New Delhi

Published by
Renu Kaul Verma for
Vitasta Publishing Pvt. Ltd.
2/15, Ansari Road, Daryaganj,
New Delhi - 110 002

ISBN 10: 81-89766-33-3
ISBN 13: 978-81-89766-33-7

Reprint 2010

Typeset & Cover Design by Vitasta Publishing Pvt. Ltd., New Delhi
Printed by Vits Press, New Delhi

To

My parents who gave me aspirations
and my in-laws who fuelled them.
My beautiful children Satwik and Vitasta from whom
I borrowed the time and space to do this book.
And Shubhendu for always being there.

Contents

Preface

The world of women is a fascinating one. It has glamour, beauty, attraction and charm. But, this book is about what lies beyond the obvious. It tells the stories of eight women who were born into average middle class families and in an era when women were bound to follow convention vis-à-vis conviction. It's about their journey against the tide and towards pursuits that were primarily considered male bastions.

These eight ladies are the light bugs of the Indian corporate jungle who lit the way for thousands to tread the path. They defied convention and broke the traditional cocoon to redefine the concept of beauty for Indian women. They reinvented beauty to mean 'beauty is what beauty does'.

Each one of them has immaculately juggled relationships without letting any piece fall. Their dreams may be made of 'Excel sheets' and 'PowerPoints', and their mind maybe focussed on the next presentation. But their heart lies with the family and employees.

These are the hands typically expected to rock the cradle but today they rule the stocks.

The stories have different hues of these women being interesting companions, compassionate daughters and daughters-in-law, super moms, considerate employers and above all, gender ambassadors.

The author has interviewed the eight ladies to revisit their childhood, the parental influences, dinner table discussions, youth pangs and what lead to their taking the path less trodden, to arrive at these fascinating stories of grit and single-mindedness. Each story is different, yet has shades that most women will identify with.

Be it the story of Kiran Mazumdar Shaw who could not get into a medical college but went on to build a pharma empire and become India's richest woman or the tale of a reluctant Kalpana Morparia who was pushed into thinking big by her mother who was widowed early in life—they all have an ordinary beginning but pan out as extraordinary success stories.

The book unveils Naina Lal Kidwai's pride on being the first Indian woman at Harvard and Neelam Dhawan's entry into a leadership position in marketing technology that was considered a male bastion. It brings out the softer self of an 'unassuming and businesslike' Vinita Bali and the cultural and artistic pursuit of a science student, Swati Piramal. It traces Ritu Kumar's journey that began from a nondescript business destination called *Bharat* to 'Brand India'. And, many would identify with the emotional turmoil of Vandana Luthra who has walked the tight rope of a typical Indian marriage and her global aspirations.

And in more ways than one, these stories stand as lighthouses for all those who are into the difficult job of parenting. Notably, all these exceptional success stories started with the parents believing in their daughters.

The book is written with the earnestness to help thousands of Indian women to believe in themselves. Success is not the caprice of fate. Those who have the fire in the belly can turn eventuality into opportunity. As the Hindi poet Dushyant Kumar puts it:

"Sirf hangama khada karna mera maksad nahi, meri koshish hai ki ye soorat badalni chahiye; mere seene mein nahi to tere seene mein sahi, ho kahin bhi aag, lekin aag jalni chahiye."

This book is an endeavour to applaud the achievements of these exceptional women who have made Indian parents look at their daughters with pride and have the same aspirations and expectations from them as they have always had from their sons.

Finally, this book is also for millions of average but special Indian women who live their lives keeping home and hearth, bringing up children and keeping their flock together. It is an ode to their contribution to our social fabric—a salute to their selfless contributions that make us who we are today. Let us not allow them to fade unsung!

ONE

The 'Bounce Back' Theory

Kiran Mazumdar Shaw

Chairman and Managing Director, Biocon Ltd.

If Kiran Mazumdar Shaw had owned up to the mediocrity that life threw at her, she wouldn't have been even a pale shadow of the woman she is today. Life tried to thwart each attempt she made. She would try to walk to the right but opportunity would pop-up the left, pushing her into directions that she didn't know ever existed, or even if she did, had no intentions to explore. So effectively, her story is that of 'bouncing back'—of striking harder when it hurts the most.

Kiran could not fight destiny but she has certainly braved quite a bit of it. She may not have got what she wanted, quite the way she wanted it. But she survived adversities one after the other to become one of the first women to walk the least-trodden path of the pharmaceutical industry in the country; with a blazing trail for many women to follow.

After 54 springs, she can only look back with baby eyes and smile at all those autumns in her life—the ones that set in when she could not get a berth at a medical school, or win a job as a brewer because of her being on the wrong side of the gender, or even her inability to turn around her dad's sick business.

She has stumbled at all those milestones to find an unexplored pathway, creating a new finish line.

Meet India's richest woman—the master brewer who continues to brew wealth for herself and her investors.

Yesteryears

Kiran's childhood was one of the most secure periods of her life, nestled in a gated community in Bangalore that housed the senior management of United Breweries where her father was the General Manager and later went on to become the Managing Director. Kiran was born on 23 March 1953 to the Mazumdars—Rasendra and Yamini—who spent a great deal of time with Kiran and her two younger brothers Ravi and Dev. They infused a fair amount of middle-class values, primarily of integrity and humility into their children. The Mazumdars believed their children should keep roots with their rich heritage. So every other summer, the family would pack their bags and hit the road for their family home at Baroda in Gujarat for bonding with relatives.

The biggest influence that Kiran remembers from her childhood is the balancing effect that her parents had on her. She inherited from her father, the art of defying convention but her mother taught her to nurture traditions and keep them alive—they both infused in her, the strength of emotional maturity that was to go a long way in modelling this first-generation entrepreneur.

"My father was full of conviction. He was straight, sometimes quite outspoken and undiplomatic and I guess I have taken after him. This is quite contrary to my mom's philosophy. She will never hurt a soul by being forthright. My father was also someone who trusted people implicitly and was often betrayed. Yet he always forgave, giving them the benefit of doubt. Another trait that I guess, I inherited from him."

Kiran was actually at the fulcrum, being guided by parents who infused their respective strengths into her subconscious during her growing years. "The greatest lesson that my father drummed into my head till he was alive was: 'Never be arrogant'. He wanted me to be humble and always remember that whatever I get—whether it is success or achievement—it is because of a set of circumstances. He warned me against walking away with all the credit. He helped me keep my head on my shoulders and it's because of him that I am still a well-rooted human being."

Kiran grew up with her father's lessons stuck like a yellow stick pad on her conscience. "Even today his lessons come back to me, especially the ones that have developed a new meaning in the management landscape in which I operate. My father used to always caution me against getting swayed by power. He would always say that there will be many people who will try to influence you by saying wonderful things but you need to be realistic about yourself and your capabilities and have a sense of fairness in every decision you take—for yourself as well as for others."

Kiran's mother holds the other end of the spectrum. Being well-versed with traditions and Hindu scriptures,

Kiran still calls up her mom to figure out what would be an auspicious date to start something new or important!

But along with steady, value-based education, the Mazumdars also gave their children lighter moments to remember them by. There was a fair amount of fun in the family, as much as an average middle-class Indian usually likes to save for and spend on. Her dad's love for golf would inevitably land the family at places like Ooty or Kashmir for holidaying where he could tee off while the others spent time chilling out. All in all, it was a normal childhood with lots of fun and no care in the world.

Amidst this charmed life, Kiran had discovered early on, her flair for leadership and keeping a flock together. "Bangalore, even at that point in time, was a very happening city. I was the eldest of a gang of kids that lived down the same lane. So I was the undisputed leader and did quite a bit of bossing around. Vijay Mallya was the boy next door and has grown up like a kid brother. It was a cushy, cozy community living."

Early life couldn't have been more benevolent—a good value system, caring parents, happy peers, and ace education. Kiran was a bright student and excelled in school. Later, she went to Mount Carmel College where she did her PUC because her maiden dream was to get into medicine.

But life can never be a constant and is a roller-coaster ride. It has its own share of crests and troughs. After some smooth sailing, Kiran had to wade through some tough weather and rough seas.

The First Big Blow

Kiran had excelled all through school and her Pre-University year and therefore had taken success for granted. Call it confidence or an overdose of it, she applied to only two medical schools, sure of her success at one of them. But ironically, she didn't make it to either!

"That was the first blow to my confidence. I tasted failure for the first time and I sure didn't relish it. I felt defeated but more than that I felt challenged. Somewhere inside, I had not accepted defeat. But at that point in time, my only recourse was to go for the second best option. So I decided to avenge destiny at a later stage and settled for science instead."

The only fallback plan was to pursue biology as a degree course, so that is what Kiran did. She took up BSc Zoology (Hons) with chemistry and botany as minors. She studied hard to excel in class but she studied harder to get the first rank in the university.

"That was my small way of answering to the challenge that the medical schools had thrown at me. It was my little way of saying--'Look what you missed out on'—I could have been a good doctor."

Once through with her degree, Kiran had the option to once again dabble with medicine. But by that time, she knew medicine was not where she wanted to be. There was more choice—she got herself enrolled into a PhD programme in University College London in genetics while also having the option to pursue applied science.

Kiran's father, who had spent a fair amount of his career in applied science, stepped in to goad her. He was a proud brewer who had spent over two decades at United Breweries, brewing successful brands like Kingfisher beer. It was his secret desire that one of his children would take up his line of expertise.

Genetic Takeover

One of Kiran's brothers, Ravi had long chosen mathematics over biology to join IIT, Powai and study engineering. Her second brother Dev was not really interested in the biological sciences so the Master Brewer urged his daughter to take a plunge and test the waters as a brewer. At that time, brewing was a fairly nascent stream in India and there weren't many professional brewers. So Kiran took on the challenge to prove herself in a vocation so unexplored by Indians and more so by women the world over.

The timing was perfect and destiny held Kiran by the hand and guided her to Australia. In those days, United Breweries used to regularly send young brewers to a programme to get them qualified to be master brewers. Kiran won a scholarship from University Women's Council (UWC) to join Ballarat University's Master Brewer's programme in Australia.

With this began the most fascinating period of Kiran's early life. "Of course, you can imagine what it would have been like to walk into a class where I was the only woman student as brewing is quite a male bastion. But I enjoyed every moment of my time there as life unfolded around me, trying me, challenging me, nudging me to be independent and excel in a man's world."

It sure was the tipping point for Kiran's confidence and self-esteem. It taught her to be independent. With each passing day, she was not just delving deeper into the magic of applied sciences but was also adding to her survival kit, the art of carrying herself with grace and confidence in a world that was still finding it difficult to accept a broader role for women.

"I learned to fend for myself and be confident amongst a group of men. That also taught me that as a woman, I do not have to feel subservient because I could equate with my male colleagues one to one."

Winds of Change

In 1975, Kiran finished her course and was ready to return home and test her newly-acquired skills. But just when Kiran had got her sails ready for the voyage, the winds at home had changed. Her father had retired from UB and had invested in a small business that was not doing well. It was draining family resources more than adding value. So from the airport, Kiran walked straight into a messy, rudderless business with her father asking for help.

A reluctant Kiran took the reigns of a sick company and got first-hand experience of trying to cope with the pressures of a faltering business.

"On hindsight, I realize that the company was badly managed and we had no professional involved to turn it around. We gave it everything—tried to get some business into the company. But the more we tried the more difficult it started to look."

Between 1976 and 1978, Kiran stayed on in Baroda trying to turn the family business around. Whilst she spent a fair amount of time trying to get some business for the sick unit, going on sales calls herself, the father-daughter duo started consulting with major breweries to keep the rations coming. But the unit was like a hole in a pot. The foundation was flawed and it was impossible to create an empire on a shaky foundation.

For the reluctant businesswoman though, this phase acted like an incubator where entrepreneurial seeds were subconsciously sown to bear fruit later.

Value of Money

It was a phase that taught Kiran to count her blessings. All the lavish holidaying was gone, outings if any, were far and few. The family was living a frugal life, saving every penny they could. After the charmed childhood, Kiran was imbibing new lessons in life. The near penury, for the first time, taught Kiran the value and significance of money.

"We would think twice before even going for a movie because all of us going together meant a lot of money and an outing would inevitably mean eating out and the fuel cost. It was the first time that we, as a family, had to think twice before spending on anything. Till then I probably knew the price of everything but the value of nothing."

Kiran was feeling restless. She joined classes to learn Hindustani classical music to sooth her nerves and connect to what she loved to do most. But, soon she knew that this was not her chosen path. The itch to move on got stronger with each passing day. As a daughter she felt responsible towards her father but as an individual, she knew she was wasting precious time.

"For two years after I came back from Australia, I had spent time doing nothing tangible and I started getting paranoid. I needed a focus in life and could not go on doing a little of this and a bit of that. So I sat with my father and we talked straight. I explained to him that it was time for me to branch out on my own."

The next day, the second biggest reality of her life struck like lightning in an already-overcast sky. Armed with one of the best degrees in brewing, she confidently went out into the world, scouting for a brewing job. But it did not take time for her to know that she was on the wrong side of the gender divide. While companies were happy to have her as a consultant, they developed cold feet when it came to trusting her with a brewery. Kiran was told that she was a woman and heading a brewery meant handling labour, being on call any time of the day or night and much more.

"Very soon, I realized that I was in the wrong country with the right credentials. The attitude of most brewing companies in India was condescending towards women. To my mind, the issues being hurled at me were a pack of nonsense but they were the reality of those times. There was a famine of confidence at the other end."

Eventually, burying her own confidence and surrendering to their lack of it, Kiran looked westwards. And she got a job in Scotland. She was all set to roll till she got this strange phone call on the day she was to leave Baroda for Delhi. Destiny at play once more! But, at times it comes with a friendly face.

The Divine Intervention

It was the morning of 25 March 1978. After a long spell of dejection, Kiran was all excited doing that last minute packing to take the Rajdhani Express to Delhi and her gateway to a roaring career as a brewer in Scotland. She planned to spend two weeks in Delhi following up on her visa and was to join her first formal assignment on April 15.

It was 8 in the morning when Kiran got a strange phone call that changed the entire course of her life... once again.

"A gentleman named Les Auchincloss who was the founder of a biotechnology company called Biocon in Ireland phoned. He had tracked me down through my friends in Australia. He was in Baroda and wanted to talk to me about a business proposal."

Auchincloss was planning to set up a company in India and he wanted Kiran to come on board and help him with it. He wanted to make an enzyme called Papain from the fruit of Papaya and also introduce some other products in the Indian market. He was looking for a brewer who had a sense of detail in these matters.

Destiny has a rude sense of humour. Obviously, Kiran's first reaction was rejection. Just when she was getting a semblance of sanity and more importantly, stability in her professional life by having a good job offer in Scotland, it made no sense to test her hands on another business in India.

Moreover, at 25, Kiran was not going to be a deterrent in Biocon's foray into India. She felt diffident about being entrusted with starting a company in a country that was not even prepared to trust her with running a brewery! Moreover, Kiran had no money to put into the venture. Auchincloss had got it all wrong.

Reading into art: Kiran loves to put her money where her heart is—in art

"I politely declined the offer but promised to introduce him to some people in Delhi who I thought would be more suitable and interested to take this up. So we decided to meet in Delhi, the following week."

Auchincloss met other prospective partners but came back to where they had started. He wanted to start small in India and wanted a partner who was entrepreneurial and who understood the business of brewing. He tried to persuade her. But Kiran would not budge. Then they made a deal. He knew Kiran's prospective employer in Scotland, so the deal was that if Kiran did not like what she was doing back in India or was not successful in the role in the first year of their partnership, she could still go back to the job in Scotland. That was a big teaser that fate handed out to her. Destiny was nudging and finally Kiran fell over the edge to walk up and down the power corridors in Delhi, trying to set up Biocon's India operations.

Instead of going to Scotland, Kiran therefore, landed in Ireland in June that year and was there for six months, training and understanding Biocon's business—in terms of its manufacturing, R&D and marketing. Handling enzymes was slightly different from being a brewer and she was learning the new ropes. The company made her travel across Europe to give her a hang of what the business was all about.

In September that year, Kiran came home once again. This time, with a great sense of deja vu, she embarked from the airport straight into setting up a new business for Biocon. The target was to get all the relevant permissions and have the company incorporated as soon as possible.

Bureaucracy without *Babudom*

In this venture, lady luck was on Kiran's side. As a woman trying to establish a foothold in the license-*raj* infested Indian business landscape, she surprised those housed in the power corridors. But they surprised her even more by being cordial and co-operative. She slowly started getting comfortable with her brushes with *babudom*.

"I remember my surprise when I saw how patronizing they were. I confided in the bureaucrats, telling them how naïve I was at trying to start a business, and more importantly, my fear to deal with corrupt practices. They assured me that my work would be done without my having to resort to any such practice!"

Kiran got the company incorporated on 29 November 1978 and chose to take the business to the city where she was born, Bangalore. She started up small in a shed with a team of two people to set up a plant for making papain. The office was in the garage of the house that she rented. There was very little capital investment involved but banks were reluctant to offer her a credit line despite a buyback arrangement with Biocon in Ireland. After several failed attempts, Canara Bank came forward to extend a credit line guaranteed by her Irish partner.

Teething Troubles

The only risk involved in the business was perceptional—that of it being headed by a woman! People did not want to touch this employer even with a barge pole.

Recruiting people became the biggest nightmare for this young woman entrepreneur. Even woman secretaries were not ready to join her even though she was ready to match market salaries. Insecurities were immense. Showing support for a distraught friend, one of Kiran's childhood friends, Pratima Rao, volunteered to act as her secretary for the first few months even though she could type with only one finger.

So for the next few months, business walked on crutches in the most amateurish manner. It was small in scale but gradually this dance of creation started looking like fun to Kiran.

"When I look at today's entrepreneurs, I feel very sad. They have to be professional from day one and have to prove themselves from the word go. Back then, we had the luxury to start in a frugal way and learn by tripping over our toes. Experimentation was the order of the day and we could have fun in building something from scratch without market pressures breathing down our necks."

But in those fluid times when business was evolving, and things were happening as and when through metamorphoses, the only things that Kiran remembers as constant were her single-mindedness, determination and passion to make it work.

"Like my earlier answer to the challenge thrown at me by the medical colleges, my single-mindedness to make Biocon work was, once again, a rebound. It was my answer to all those people who had refused to trust me with a brewery. It was again retaliation to those who did not accept me as an equal in business because of my gender."

Crack Team

The wheel of time changed in 1983 when India was gradually waking up to entrepreneurship. Earlier, Biocon had failed to attract talent as most parents would never let their bright ones join a fledgling business. They would rather have them live a life of a struggling medic or an engineer or at best join the government. The risk-taking environment did not exist. But the winds of change were blowing and India's success in software and services was infusing confidence into youngsters to test uncharted waters.

Kiran found some interesting and like-minded people who were willing to take that plunge with her. Her first professional recruitment was her CFO, Murali Krishnan who continues to hold that responsibility till date. Then came her R&D Head Shrikumar Suryanarayan who sacrificed an offer to pursue a PhD programme at an Ivy League college in the US to start up Biocon's research division. Ajay Bharadwaj joined her next to take up marketing responsibility by quitting a large pharmaceutical company in India. Arun Chandavarkar, Biocon's Chief Operating Officer, returned from MIT in Boston USA and joined Biocon despite lucrative offers from larger companies including one from HLL. It was an interesting time and the team got into a huddle to create something that was new to the sector and in a way, also new to the country. The crack team that showed confidence in the potential of a 'fledgling of an idea' called Biocon stays on till date, except the marketing head who moved on to become an entrepreneur himself.

And thus was born a family—the Biocon clan that decided to battle it out together through thick and thin. Building the company was like raising a child—demanding, mostly rewarding but at other times testing. They all put their shoulders to the wheel and sure got bruised for a long time.

"We saw some very tough times. At times, we delayed taking our salaries so that we could rally around pressures. There were times when we didn't take increments to keep the business wheel in motion."

And then one fine morning in 1989, the Irish company was acquired by Unilever. Overnight Biocon had a change of parentage. For the next ten years, the somewhat interesting relationship of the big and mighty Unilever with this tiny biotechnology company, operating from the outskirts of Bangalore, continued.

For the company, the acquisition was a God-sent opportunity to learn and evolve. It was the most important phase in Biocon's life-cycle because the tiny entrepreneurial venture, for the first time, started to professionalize on mass scale. Biocon imbibed all the good systems and best practices of the MNC parent. It became process-oriented and learned never to compromise on quality.

"Going through the audits made us realize just how good we were. Association with Unilever also got us into the patenting culture and we learned the nuances of the intellectual property space."

Kiran and John: Partners in life and business

Mama's daughter: With Yamini

Then Mr Shaw Showed up

By 1991, Biocon was doing fine and Kiran was content with the way things were shaping up professionally. She was finally warming up to being a businesswoman. Also, now there was some time to socialize. And it was then that Kiran met a friend, who would eventually turn out to be a long-term associate and finally her partner in business and in life. John Shaw was posted in Bangalore as head of Madura Coats and Kiran started meeting him at social networking events that abounded the teeming city of Bangalore.

"Gradually, we discovered that we had a lot of common interests. We both were into art and John was keen to be introduced to Indian art. So, I took it upon myself to introduce him to the Indian art scene. We visited art exhibitions and met artists together."

As a masterstroke of destiny, Kiran had just started testing her hand at golf and John was an avid golfer. So weekend golf cemented the bond. Even though both travelled a lot, they started spending a fair amount of their time together whenever they were in Bangalore, doing things they both loved most.

"He was a very good friend and I found that John was a great sounding board. At the top, you are always very lonely. In taking certain critical decisions, I felt a very strong urge to speak to somebody who was impartial and wise."

Since Shaw was from a multinational company, he helped Kiran to get a peek into the MNC psyche—the way they think, the way they perceive things. This came very handy for Kiran who was running a smaller company that had to live under the shadows of a big brother like Unilever.

A few years later, Shaw was posted in Europe. Within a month of his leaving, the duo realized what a bad idea it had been not to take the relationship to the logical conclusion. They had spent seven years of togetherness without thinking of spending their lives together. It was high time they got married. So they tweaked their lives a bit here and there and walked down the aisle.

"I told John, now that we are going to get married, one of us will have to give up the job and it's not going to be me. John was only too pleased to take early retirement from Coats Viyella and join me at Biocon."

Bringing the Biocon Baby Home

Kiran's personal life was showing signs of settling down, but there were issues that needed immediate attention on the professional front. In 1998, the time for her marriage coincided with the time when Unilever decided to exit the biotech business worldwide, of which Biocon was a small part. But Kiran was not going to put the kid on the block. She decided she would buy the shares back from Unilever. Kiran turned to her would-be-husband for help and he obliged.

"John always teases me. He had always heard stories of Indian men getting a dowry at the time of marriage. But in our case, he walked into our marriage by parting with his lifetime savings to buy the shares back from Unilever. His funniest one-liner is: 'Contrary to the Indian tradition, Kiran completely cleaned me out!'"

John Shaw sold his prime and most prized possession—a house in London—and became the first venture capitalist for the Indian biotechnology sector. Fortunately, his decision to invest in Kiran as well as her company was to bear rich dividends. He and Kiran brought the Biocon baby home and Biocon became a hundred per cent privately-owned company. So for a change, behind this successful woman there is a man.

Bicon did go on to become the greatest pursuit of the couple after they realized that it was too late in the day to have a baby of their own. "I realized that Biocon was as great a responsibility as it is to raise a baby. I sure am fond of kids but that vacuum is completely filled by my niece and nephews who are adorable and the apples of my eye."

John proved to be a secure and understanding husband and participated in his wife's success without qualms. He was never intimidated by the power that Kiran wielded in her circles. The paucity of time that the two usually spend together is more than made up by their breezy visits to Barcelona, Spain that remains the first love for both.

The Shaws like to spend Christmas or the year-end in Canada or the US where Kiran's brothers live or holidaying at common destinations where they can unwind with their families.

Pushing the Envelope

The lack of anchoring responsibilities at home gave the two more time to invest in business that was, by now, their own. They channelized all their efforts towards working on a new set of targets and setting new challenges for themselves and the company.

"I had started thinking about the future and we wanted to become a billion dollar company. One way to do that was to attain a market capitalization of one billion dollars. But at that time, we were not so concerned about the bourses. We decided to work towards revenues of one billion dollars."

That was 1998. Kiran decided to give themselves 15 years to get to \$1 billion in revenues. That was an aggressive goal given that Biocon's revenue at that time was hovering around Rs 70 crore. Even if Biocon captured the largest chunk of the global enzymes business, they would still fall short of the \$1 billion goal. So something else had to be done.

The company realized that enzymes were a good way to begin. But if they continued to make only enzymes, they would be working in a self-limiting space. The total global market for enzymes was about Rs 7,000 crore. A major portion of this market comprised commodity enzymes. Biocon could not aspire for even a 15 per cent share of that market as they dealt in specialty enzymes which in itself was a mere Rs 1,000-crore opportunity.

So they went back to the drawing board and looked at a path that was different. Pharmaceuticals were obviously the most logical progression. And within the somewhat-cluttered pharmaceutical space in India, Biocon decided to focus on biopharmaceuticals. The change of strategy worked for Biocon that moved from revenues of Rs 70 crore in 1998 to become a Rs 500-crore company in 2004 when it finally went public.

But all this did not come without new learning. Pharma was a completely different ball game when compared to manufacturing enzymes. Biocon had to learn the regulatory ropes for launching pharma products.

"Since our main markets were the US and Europe that are even more regulated, the biggest challenge was to meet the stringent regulatory criteria imposed by these markets. That was the confidence building phase because we started in 1998 and by the end of 2000 we actually got inspected by US FDA and by January 2001 we were qualified."

After this, there was no looking back for Biocon. The company was the first to discover the statin opportunity that went on to become a major success story for the company. Unfortunately, that success was replicable and others jumped into the fray making it less attractive for the pioneers.

Eye for Future

But that hardly bothered Kiran. The vision she had for the company was crystal clear. Generics was always supposed to be a means to the end and not an end in itself. At that point in time, while the Indian market had big players like Ranbaxy and Dr Reddy's that boasted of a very strong generic focus, Kiran wanted Biocon to be different.

"We wanted to differentiate into new molecules but you cannot jump into new molecules without understanding the pharmaceutical business as a whole. Unfortunately, we got labelled as a generics company because we started with them and people refused to buy into our strategy of developing novel and proprietary drug molecules. We had spelt out our intent even during our IPO where the prospectus clearly said that generics are not the be all and end all for us. It's just a way of getting into new molecules."

Biocon gradually went on to in-license and partner a number of discovery-led programmes. It had a strong insulin programme so insulin became a molecule which was Biocon's next big bet after statins. This time, they went beyond the concept of insulin being a generic; they decided to embark on a novel 'Oral Insulin' programme. It started as a partnered programme with Nobex, a US based Biotech company which had a proprietary technology to deliver peptides orally but later Biocon acquired the IP assets of Nobex and came to fully own the oral insulin programme. The company also partnered with a Cuban research institute with whom they started developing monoclonal antibodies for cancer and inflammatory diseases. Through this partnership, Biocon rolled out its first proprietary molecule, BIOMAb-EGFR for cancer, into the Indian market. However, the company still gets supported financially by a number of generic products like insulin, statins, immunosuppressants and other bio-generics.

"In the next five years, we expect Biocon to be a very different company. We would largely have proprietary products. We have a rich pipeline of new molecules under various stages of development. We are hopeful that many of these will make it to the market in the years ahead."

Ms Richie Rich

After Biocon went public in 2004, Kiran Mazumdar Shaw emerged the richest woman in India. She was valued at $ 400 million then and her wealth today hovers between $500-600 million. She may be Ms Richie

Kiran was awarded the *Padma Bhushan* in 2005 for her pioneering efforts in Industrial Biotechnology

Rich, but she is not the kind to name her two dogs as Dollar and Euro. And it's a label that embarrasses her more than anything.

"I don't like to be called the richest woman. Initially, it made me uneasy and turn and twist in my seat whenever they introduced me in that manner. But now I have learned to accept it as an acknowledgement for the fact that I have created high value which is what I am really proud of. If wealth creation and creation of value for the company, its employees and the investors through business is to be perceived as being rich, I most humbly accept the label."

When people introduce me as the richest woman of India, I can sense what is on their minds—'She doesn't even look it'. Really, I feel more honoured and comfortable being recognized as a successful businesswoman."

Kiran spends a lot of time explaining to people how her wealth oscillates on an everyday basis. "I can lose or gain millions in a day and that is frightful. But I don't let it bother me."

However, Kiran has accepted the responsibility with grace. She has learned to look at it more through the prism of philosophy, looking at it as a position where she can influence change in the lives of other women, letting them believe that they can also do it.

Kiran is among the 40 richest Indians (according to Forbes 2007). But it's not just her wealth that makes her rich. Kiran has received an honorary Doctorate of Science from her alma mater—Ballarat University Australia—in recognition of her preeminent contributions to the field of Biotechnology. Recently, she also received an Honorary Doctorate from the Manipal Academy of Higher Education (MAHE), in recognition of her outstanding achievements in biotechnology and industrial enzymes.

Even though the business community has showered her with an endless list of awards, her most-cherished awards are the *Padma Shri* that was conferred upon her in 1989, followed by the *Padma Bhushan* in 2005, presented to her by the President of India for her pioneering efforts in Industrial Biotechnology.

But for Kiran, she still remains the first-generation woman entrepreneur who seized the opportunity to create wealth with her unfazed determination and a team of people who trusted her enough to take risks that were bold but well-calculated.

Money Matters

For the richest woman in India, Kiran is a fairly simple person and she certainly does not sleep with lots of notes under her mattress or jewellery in her loft.

"My financial advisor often tells me, people can have a good laugh at my expense if they peep into my bank statements. All my money is in my shares. And I have no plans to cash out and exit from the company."

So while people would see Kiran carrying the company around with her for a long time, they are unlikely to spot her walking away with her pot of gold.

"I am not an extravagant person and the last thing that I intend doing in this lifetime is to flaunt my wealth.

My husband always says that one good thing about me is that I am never interested in big time spending— be it on clothes or jewellery or all those rich and famous things that people love to flaunt."

Kiran's idea of fashion too is fairly simple. One would not see Kiran turning out shabby at any event but she is not the type to dabble heavily into expensive designer stuff. She has a versatile dress sense and feels as comfortable in casual kurtas as she is in formal jackets.

"I appreciate good jewellery and love to see it on others. That does not mean I will hop on to the next shop to pick up something similar. I like pearls and one would see me wearing them quite often. But that's about it. I will never weigh more because of the amount of jewellery I flaunt."

But when it comes to investing, Kiran loves to put her money where her heart is—in art. While Kiran invested a lot of time on painting in her younger years, she can now keep up with the love by just getting enough time to pick a good piece wherever she sees one.

Outside business too, Kiran believes in better utilization of wealth and not pursuing useless pursuits. A major part of her money is going into philanthropy. Kiran started Biocon Foundation where she is building a rural health care scheme based on a micro-health insurance system. This also involves building clinics and connecting them to anchor hospitals. This is a partnered initiative with Dr Devi Shetty's Narayana Hrudayalaya Hospital where the main objective is to deliver affordable health care to rural and underprivileged sections of the society. Kiran has recently announced a partnership with Dr Devi Shetty in promoting 'health cities' across the country to deliver affordable health care.

Hard Shell–Soft Core

All is never hunky dory at the top. Kiran's success has put her in a position of responsibility where she is ranked among all the leading business people in the country. She is always in the limelight and sometimes has to face the ire or sadism of unhealthy competition or irresponsible media.

When it comes to handling sentiments, there certainly are a few things that Kiran would like to work on. Under the hard façade lies a soft person who gets perturbed by the slightest of provocations and would brood over them for hours. Recently, when a leading daily published a picture of Kiran with Rajasthan Chief Minister Vasundhara Raje taken from an angle that distorted the facts, Kiran was livid and hurt. It was terrible for her friend in politics as the picture was used by her opponents to mislead the electorate.

"What may have looked like a joke in bad taste to the media fraternity and others, cost my friend some very precious votes. I still have to learn to take unfair attacks in my stride. I need to shed this over-sensitivity."

Fortunately, Kiran has friends who would rationalize with her and comfort her in her time of need. She keeps a very close coterie of friends that include the old gang from Bangalore—Vijay Mallya and Sunil Alagh included. She also has a close set of girlfriends like Nilima Rovshen who is with an NGO, The Wadhwani Foundation. Then there is Meeru Pai, Poornima Dhawan, Leena Singh and Rini Kumar who know her and understand where she comes from.

"I have learned that one will never be lonely at the top if one has good friends, family and close colleagues."

Feminism: Handling All Things Male

With women in business being far and few, men inadvertently say patronizing things about other women. Kiran believes that men still find it difficult to see and accept women outside the framework that society has conventionally worked out for them.

Kiran gets paranoid when people walk up to her and ask questions like: "Do you think women can have the same ambitions as men? Don't you think men are much more ambitious, aggressive and go getting? My only answer to them is—Listen I have built a pretty reasonable sized business and I think I am as ambitious as any man. Women can win; they can compete with any man.

I don't think I am a feminist who believes that you have to outdo men in everything there is. I just believe that the world should offer equal opportunities to people of all caste, creed and gender."

When it comes to both feminism and entrepreneurship, Kiran's mother has proved where the genes have travelled from. After Mr Mazumdar passed away in 1993, she picked up the strings of her life at age 65 by keeping herself busy growing organic and exotic vegetables in her backyard in Bangalore. Her target audience was five stars hotels and the NRI community living in Bangalore. In more recent times, she started running a laundry service and has all major airlines as her clients.

"I have seen her clients sit with her for hours sipping their coffee and discussing their times and life. She has discovered her own niche in life."

Beyond Success

Of late, Kiran's friends may be complaining about her being low-key. The party animal seems to have become a bit reclusive and she admits she does not enjoy endless parties where nobody seems to be making sensible conversation anymore. Big parties, with halls full of people, have become more of a chore.

"I admit there was a time when I could party all night. But I guess every human evolves and so do one's preferences in life. Glamour comes with an expiry date and beyond it there is only the internal life force that keeps one going. I would rather spend time with a smaller group of people whose company I enjoy than end up in a senseless crowd."

Her priorities have changed too. "When I am not spending time at home with John and our two dogs or unwinding listening to Hindustani or western classical music, I am thinking about the life beyond this success. I guess I want to change the world in my own small way. But for that it was important to get to a position of responsibility and credibility."

Having created her share of wealth and more importantly earned her piece of respect in the professional world, this first-generation woman entrepreneur is looking forward to making this world a better place to be. And she sure seems to be the chosen one.

"Coming from where I am, I have got from life much more than I could even have imagined. I think now it is time to give back to the society. If there are lives that I can touch by kind words or deeds, I better do it now."

* * * * *

TWO

The 'Make it Happen' Lady

Kalpana Morparia

Vice Chair for ICICI's Insurance,
Security and Asset Management Business

This is the story of a dreamy-eyed girl who thought that high school education was enough to last for a lifetime. It is the tale of an average Gujarati lass for whom painted nails, getting married and having lots of kids was as big as dreams could get. For her, the most valuable certificate of merit came from the mirror on the wall and the best things in life were showcased only in the big glitzy world of Bollywood.

Kalpana Morparia nursed no pretence of being a student who wanted to be among the 'top three' in her class nor did she want her name in the school's hall of fame. She did not think women were carved out to make a career. Her idea of a complete woman was to be a well-looked after wife with unmatched housekeeping skills.

In a way, this idea came with the genes and her upbringing. Kalpana was born on 30 May 1949 in a traditional Gujarati background. Her maternal great grandfather and paternal grandfather had migrated to Mumbai. In that time and age, Gujarati girls were taught the ropes of keeping a family very early on in life. The better they were at house chores; brighter was the future that awaited them after marriage.

Life, however, is all about wringing destinies to make something out of nothing or vice-versa. So, it gave Kalpana's story the right twist. This Gujarati lass grew up to raise money for the Industrial Credit and Investment Corporation of India Limited (ICICI) and list it on the New York Stock Exchange (NYSE) in September 1999. She spearheaded the merger of ICICI with ICICI Bank in May 2002 and handled the highly complex restructuring of the somewhat jinxed Dabhol power project. Somewhere along her 32-year stint with the organization, ICICI has almost become the surname for Kalpana Morparia who is now Vice Chairperson for ICICI's Insurance, Security and Asset Management businesses and Chief Strategy and Communications Officer for the ICICI Group.

The Paradox

Kalpana's lack of ambition was more than compensated by her mother, Laxmi Tanna, who had lost her husband very early in life. Thus, she had queen-sized aspirations for her two daughters. Having tasted the vagaries of life at an early stage, she was singularly focused on making her daughters find their ground before they even thought of marriage. However, her ambition turned out to be Kalpana's worst nightmare.

"I lost my father very early in life and I was the youngest in the family. My mother played the most dominant role in our lives. Whilst I may be accused of being bias, I daresay that she was the most wonderful lady in the world. I lost her a few months ago and that has left a great void in our lives. She was beautiful, gracious and competent but did not really have the benefit of academics."

She had suffered much in life because she was not educated, so she constantly tried to drill into Kalpana's tiny head the value of becoming independent and self-sufficient. The more her mother prodded Kalpana to focus on studies, the more she thought about how best to finish school and settle down as a homemaker.

"I grew up in an environment which constantly exhorted me to study rather than think about marriage or any deviations. Paradoxically, that is exactly what I thought most about."

The reasons for the lack of seriousness probably stemmed from the fact that Kalpana was the youngest in the family and grew up as a somewhat-pampered sibling. Being brought up without a father also meant getting lavish and sometimes unsolicitous attention as the 'baby of the house'.

Shielded Schooling

Kalpana's mother had witnessed insecurity at an early stage so she was paranoid about shielding her daughter from any distractions that could make her lose focus.

Initially, she sent Kalpana to the Hill Grange School in Mumbai that was a co-educational school but soon shifted her to Walsingham House School for she thought that her daughter would grow up much more shielded in a girls school.

"I used to be in the top 10-12 in the class and never ever exerted myself into doing any better. I was very active in drama and creative stuff and participated in dancing, acted and even directed a play. And of course, I was a big Bollywood fan. But that was about it. Academics had a limited role to play and there was no clear cut focus in my life."

The fact that Kalpana could not think beyond the conventional mould was also because she was surrounded by friends who belonged to wealthy families and all that they thought about was getting married and settling down. So her childhood flowered under two contradictory influences.

"The thought of trying to strive for a career was not even distant in my mind. But my mother was equally determined in making me at least self-sufficient."

Back in the 60s, any mother who wished a career for her daughter could never visualize beyond her girl donning a white apron, with a proud stethoscope hanging down the neck. Becoming a doctor was the ultimate definition of success for women. Naturally, Kalpana's mother wanted her to become a doctor.

"I passed out of school at 16. Most of my friends wanted to wait till 18 to get married and they migrated to St Xavier's College for studying arts that was a very popular discipline at that time. I had done fairly well in science even with my indifferent attitude. So my mother pushed me into a science college, brushing aside my protests on how I was missing out on all good things in life by not going to Xavier's with my friends. Despite all fretting and fuming, I was marched off to Sophia College for Women where I could study science and more importantly, I would study only with girls."

Kalpana walked into a four-year science regime but her determination about not becoming a medic matched her mother's perseverance to push her into it. She pursued Bachelors in Science with Chemistry as the primary specialization and Microbiology as a subsidiary.

"At the end of the second year of the degree course, you had to make your choice on whether you wanted to study medicine or not. I was quiet determined not to become a doctor. The very thought of it put me off. But I knew I would fight a losing battle if I confided in my mother. So in some ways, I deliberately understudied so that I would not make it to the cut off. Fortunately, I got one or two per cent less than the cut off percentage required for studying medicine. Mom had no choice but to allow me to graduate in science."

Concluding Ceremony

College was great fun. Kalpana was a happy-go-lucky young woman and unlike the youngsters today, who dress sloppily, her gang was the one who took pride in dressing up. They would save money to lunch out and took special pleasure in bunking college to see a movie.

On the day her graduation examinations got over, Kalpana made a little ceremony of putting a formal full stop to her academic pursuits.

"I wanted to make sure that everyone got the message that I was done with studies. Being a graduate was a big thrill...the movie *Graduate* had just released then and that gave us an additional high. So we were preening at having accomplished the impossible."

Her graduation was a landmark in more than one way. If Kalpana's professors track down what she is doing today, they would only accept it as the Almighty's miracle. Even her teachers in school, especially her Hindi teacher would always say: "This girl will not do anything in life...all she can think of is brushing her hair all day long."

Braving all odds, Kalpana graduated in 1970 and two days after her results, she got a job to teach at Manav Mandir School. She taught for a couple of months and realized that she could not go on as she had laryngitis. Speaking for extended periods of time made her vocal cords to swell.

"That was manna from the heaven. I thought that was it. Destiny had taken me into its folds and now I could sit at home and do nothing!"

Of Shattered Illusions

Illusions have a way of breaking soundlessly. Kalpana's ultimate desire in life had been to keep a house and get accustomed to being a housewife completely. However, it just took her ten months at home to understand that she would die of boredom if all she had to do was cook and keep a house. Life played its little game again and Kalpana was soon weaning to get out and do something more challenging.

After her aborted stint at the school, it was too late for her to join a post graduation course as it was two months too late for any admissions.

"Being at home, every household chore fell in my lap and I was bored into tears. What I thought could be the most fulfilling experience for a woman turned out to be one of the most painful periods of my life. For the next ten months, I was at the drudge at home."

She looked for ways to fill time, enrolled in a cookery class with Tarla Dalal. "That was fantastic and she completely changed the way I looked at cooking. But that was only one part and not the sum total of life for me any more."

Kalpana started looking for a tiny window to peep out at life. The nearest one was the one that opened into her sister's life. Kalpana's elder sister had studied law and was going to join a solicitor's office. So for want of doing something better, in 1971, Kalpana enrolled for a day law school in the Government Law College, Mumbai.

"Initially, I did not treat the three-year course with any more respect than with what I had treated school or college. Fortunately, around that time a lot was happening and the Indian Constitution was constantly being amended by the government."

The first serious thought beyond fun, partying and Bollywood struck Kalpana while she was still in the first year of her law studies. The Constitution was being amended to severely curtail certain fundamental rights pertaining to property. Consequently, a movement originated at the Government Law College and the students took out a procession. Kalpana participated in it—her first public involvement. Post the movement, she started enjoying law and though she bunked classes, she applied herself to the subject much better.

Marriage Finally Happened

Kalpana had for long dreamt of the day of her marriage but when she really walked into it, it caught her unprepared as it was scheduled barely a month before the examinations of her second year at law. By then, Kalpana's outlook about life had undergone a complete change and she knew that she would not walk into the marriage at the cost of walking out on her law degree.

Her husband Jaisingh (Jai), who was a friend of her brother's and who she had known for sometime, seconded Kalpana on her seriousness about appearing for her examination. Even though she married into a typical conservative Gujarati family that had a dozen members staying together, they supported her pursuit and encouraged her to finish the course.

"Jai has been very supportive all through. I would go to a friend's house every morning and we would study together. Since I had applied myself to it, I fared very well in the examinations."

By then, Kalpana had grown much beyond her dream of just cooking and keeping a house.

Immediately after she finished law-graduation in 1974, she joined the law firm Matubhai Jamietram and Madon. The firm had a policy of not paying unless one decided to do articles but Kalpana was more interested in the exposure. Within a few months, she moved on to Bhai Shankar Kanga and Company where she got a chance to work with a fine lawyer who was a specialist in litigation.

This was the time when she was toying with the idea of signing in and taking up a full-fledged law career or joining a corporate house. She applied to Hindustan Levers for a job, was interviewed but it did not work out. Around the same time, someone informed her about the Industrial Credit and Investment Corporation (ICICI), which had a good in-house legal department.

"I had never studied commerce. All I understood of ICICI was that it is a developmental financial institution that gave money to the industry and needed lawyers."

If it would not have been for the Reader's Digest, Kalpana would probably have meandered into becoming a solicitor. One day while sitting in a 'BEST' bus, she was reading the magazine that she feels "is always exhorting you into doing something. I read something that stuck in my mind. It said: *Don't leave for tomorrow what you need to do today.*" The first thing she did when she got home was write out an application to ICICI for joining their legal department as there was no formal procedure for applying at that time.

The company responded after three months and that started the series of her interviews with the corporation. She went to meet the legal adviser who interviewed her but said they were embarking upon a formal application procedure and that she would have to respond to an advertisement when the company called for applications.

In those days when ICICI was a 343-strong organization, even an entry-level candidate was required to meet the entire top management. Therefore, the process that she initiated in January fructified in October and Kalpana finally joined the 20-strong legal department of ICICI in November 1975.

"On the day of the final interview, I told the room full of ICICI's top management that I had waited enough for this position. I needed to know if I stood a chance or was I required to move on with life. They all smiled and said I was in."

The role was critical. Since the corporation gave financial assistance, the moment it was sanctioned, the legal department would come into play to see if everything was in order for the funds to be disbursed. And those were the days when even those companies that had nothing on the ground used to tap the capital market.

"I took to it like a fish to water, not as a mundane job but as a party that felt equally enthused by the spirit of the people who were asking for money to start a project or to put up a factory. I felt completely involved in their aches and pains and that completely changed my orientation towards life."

Maybe there had always been a pent-up desire to do something substantial but that got fully unleashed in the environment that ICICI provided Kalpana with.

Up the Ladder

Unlike the career progression today—which is pretty much on the fast track—it was different back in the 70s. Typically, for the first five to six years, one would be required to work 'hands on' as a dealing officer on the field and then graduate to the first supervisory level.

"There are lots of things that fit the perspective only when viewed in hindsight. I joined in November and worked six days a week because I loved what I was doing. Barely 15 months into the job, I was asked to coordinate the work done by our southern regional office. Although it went under the euphemism of 'coordinate', the work in some ways was the first supervisory role. I resisted it vehemently as I was thoroughly enjoying my field job and was too naïve to understand the significance of moving on to a supervisory level."

Kalpana was moved to tears but the organization was relentless. Today, she can only look back and thank those seniors who had the vision to recognize the managerial spark in her and literally bully her into her first supervisory role. The assignment completely changed her approach. Earlier, it was about the work that she was doing herself, now it was all about facilitating a task for others. It was a milestone for her as it taught her how to interact with others, build teams and influence people very early in her career. It gave her an ultimate ambition: "*How can I make something happen*?"

From here on, it was a fascinating journey of Kalpana's growth with the brand called ICICI. In 1981, significant changes were materializing at the corporation. Till then, since ICICI was a lending-focused organization, all the legal work that was being done was focused on the asset side of the balance sheet. In the early 80s, liabilities started emerging as a challenge. Exploring innovative ways of resource raising became centre stage.

"We were lenders of foreign currency as India had not opened up and for a company to even import equipment, it needed a financial institution to co-ordinate the funding. It was time to tap foreign resources to channelize them into Indian industry. For ICICI, that side of business was very thinly manned. It was complex in terms of execution as it meant dealing with Forex regulation and laws and listing norms across countries etc."

The organization needed a dedicated legal resource and Kalpana got sucked into it. In 1981, ICICI embarked upon its bond raising in the overseas market. It was actually the second fund raising, the first being a small Swiss bond issue. However, this one was to be of a handsome sum of $30 million. It was to be listed on Singapore and Luxembourg stock exchanges and the exercise was very complicated as it was guaranteed by the Government of India.

"That was a watershed as I got exposed to policy frame-work, bureaucracy, foreign investment bankers, foreign lawyers, regulators and it completely opened up new vistas for me. Since it was a very critical assignment for us, I was directly working with the joint MD and the chairman was overseeing it. The exercise gave me a lot of exposure to the top management."

With this first brush with the liability side of the balance sheet at ICICI, Kalpana was to stay associated with it for a long time in one capacity or another.

The Guiding Hand of Providence

In 1982, the ICICI went through a reorganization where the legal department was dismantled and attached to the business groups. The idea was that everybody needs to be a generalist where they would originate the loan appraisal, document it and monitor it until repayment. But the organization still needed a core legal function to handle the liability part of the balance sheet and hand-hold it on other legal advisory and litigation work.

"I was one of the four-member team that was not put into the general pool. That was a landmark for if I had moved into the general management cadre at that time, I would have completely lost touch with my core strength. In the new capacity, every new product or institution that ICICI came in touch with had a very active involvement from our team—whether it was about outsourcing the canteen facility or raising equity capital, a lawyer was always required."

In a way, Kalpana's exposure to the top management as a legal colleague in most projects undertaken by the company became instrumental in highlighting her capabilities. Even after the change of guard where Mr SS

Nadkarni moved on and Mr N Vaghul came in to head the institution as the seventh chairperson, Kalpana found herself in the centre of activity.

Incidentally, during her various assignments, she also got closely associated with KV Kamath, who eventually came in as the Managing Director and CEO of ICICI. The association started when Mr Kamath was the head of the leasing function. It was the time when the leasing concept was so new to India that they had to dig into regulations to see what relevant law would apply to the business. Living through those teething troubles had given them an opportunity to respect each others' capabilities. Later Mr Kamath moved on to head the liability section which is now called treasury where Kalpana again got to work with him closely as a law colleague.

One Step at a Time

Interestingly, when Kalpana joined corporate India, it was a different ball game. In the old ICICI of the 70s and the early 80s, irrespective of her close working association with the top management and handling critical portfolios, she had to walk up the hierarchical path. Assignments may have meant Kalpana reporting several times directly to the chairman but her title was still deputy manager. Therefore, for the first 15 years of her career with ICICI, it took her five years to cross each supervisory grade from 1990 to 2001 and thereon she got a promotion every two years. In those days, getting a promotion every two years was a big accomplishment—something to brag about.

On the day her graduation examinations got over, Kalpana made a little ceremony of putting a formal full stop to her academic pursuits

Nevertheless, the organization did help her in honing her skills for bigger responsibilities. Since Kalpana was associated with resource raising, in 1991, ICICI sent her for three months to a New York-based law firm called Davis Polk and Wardwell to work as a temporary foreign associate for her to get accustomed to the legal and practical aspects of issuing capital in the US markets.

"It was a very good exposure and it opened my mind to international best practices. Incidentally, it was my first visit to the US. The only regret is that I was 40 at that time. Had I gone ten years earlier, I would have taken a career break and studied law and worked there for a while before coming back."

The period from 1992 to 1996 was a very exciting period for the entire corporate sector in India as the country embarked on the much-needed and eagerly-awaited liberalization of the Indian economy. These were the most exciting times to be a part of the financial sector where, for the first time, creative and entrepreneurial forces were unleashed in the board rooms of key private players.

ICICI was leading several of these changes with its foray into commercial banking, investment banking, brokerage and asset management. Being an integral part of the core legal team, Kalpana participated and in several cases drove these initiatives from the legal side. Negotiating skills and timely and relentless execution skills that were honed over several years at ICICI were invaluable in these exciting and challenging assignments. Some of the more critical assignments included joint venture negotiations with foreign joint venture partners like JP Morgan.

It was under this backdrop that ICICI Bank was born in January 1994. Kalpana worked towards getting it incorporated on January 5 to make it coincide with the birth of ICICI.

Lawyer to a Corporate Leader

Six months before Mr Kamath came in as Managing Director and CEO and the announcement of his appointment was made; he started frequenting Mumbai every month for interactions with the team. It was 1996, and by then, ICICI was like a family to Kalpana.

Kalpana's long association with both the ICICI family as well as Mr Kamath emboldened her to discuss with him topics that could not be called her core areas of responsibility. It was the time when the organization was facing a liquidity challenge and interest rates were almost touching 17-18 per cent. She kept stressing upon the funding challenge and how the organization needed more middle-level talent to tide over the crisis.

But what started with informal briefing sessions culminated into what Kalpana had not really asked for. Mr Kamath asked her to head the treasury function.

"When it comes to Mr Kamath, one never says no but he could see the shock on my face and he didn't want to discuss it any further."

In fact, he had also hinted that if Kalpana nursed dreams of being a part of the board of the company, he would not be able to do much if she did not become multi-disciplinary. It was a painful decision to move out of a discipline where you are a queen bee into a totally new area. Moreover, Kalpana was the only top manager in ICICI who had no formal management training.

"I consulted my friends Mr Bhojani (my immediate boss at that time and long-time friend and mentor) and Mr Chaukar (Managing Director of ICICI Securities) and both told me, this was not the time to back out. I was a little apprehensive about moving into a new area but more than that, I was reluctant to give up the comfort zone of my law discipline. However, I went on to accept the assignment and the idea was that we will find someone to substitute me in the legal department."

The company could not find someone for the position, so in the interim it was decided that Kalpana would work with both functions and would have two bosses to report to, one on the treasury side and the other for the legal function. But this was not to end here. A few weeks before Mr Kamath was to take over, he called up from Indonesia at 7 in the morning to say: "Kalpana, in addition to treasury, I want the entire communication function to be handled by you—media, analysts, investors, rating agencies and I want you to handle the regulatory interface as well." This also included being the brand manager for the ICICI brand.

"To me, media till then meant reading the newspapers and listening to the news. He wanted a full-fledged communication department and the external stakeholders under one person. Now, not only did I have the challenge of handling the treasury but I also had much more on my platter than I could possibly chew. But my motto being: 'how to make it happen', I tried to work around it."

Bereft of any formal knowledge in economics, commerce, brand management or even public relations, Kalpana found herself in the midst of a job bouquet that required her to handle all these functions and many more. But that hardly unnerved her. She banked upon her practical acumen.

"I have always believed that specialists tend to make their subject more complicated than it actually is. One of the things that you need to excel in as a leader—be it in any function— is to select the right team by picking up the right people. You can never be, nor are you required to be, the fountain head of all knowledge."

She got cracking first with the task of team building. She cherry-picked Nachiket Mor who had taken a four-year career break to do his doctorate at Wharton and was back with the asset side of the business. Kalpana took him into the treasury side. She gathered six stalwarts in her team—for foreign currency resources, rupee resources, capital raising, planning, budgeting and regulatory interface.

Having built a crack team, she started to do what she does best, that is, thinking and strategizing. Thereafter, she focused on implementation of plans with the help of the specialists.

"I work best when I feel constrained. Hence, I thoroughly enjoyed my role in terms of challenges that were faced by the resources side. There were a lot of regulatory and policy changes that had to be undertaken to bring efficiency into the system of resource raising. Willy-nilly, my legal knowledge came handy…all training that I had got in managing teams helped me to break ice with both external and internal stake holders." Within two months of Mr Kamath's joining, ICICI raised equity capital of $200 million through an issue of Global Depository Receipts (GDRs) in the international markets.

"With media, the first interaction made my stomach muscles knot but when I chatted with them, I realized they were working under the same competitive pressure as we were. So it was not out of any particular agenda that they were probing…They were probing because they wanted to beat their competition to a piece of news. That made me ease up a bit and many of them went on to become very good friends."

Milestones on Way

1996 till 2001 was a watershed period in the history of ICICI and so was it for Kalpana in more ways than one. As a core member of ICICI senior management, Kalpana was involved and also spearheaded multiple capital raisings; both debt and equity in the domestic and international markets. It was also the time when she was involved in the mergers of SCICI (a specialized lending institution promoted by ICICI) and two non-banking companies engaged in the retail business of lending and distribution, and finally the acquisition of Bank of Madura by ICICI Bank. Meanwhile, ICICI diversified into consumer credit and other retail businesses.

As a part of brand management, Kalpana was required to reposition ICICI as a universal bank providing the entire gamut of financial products to corporate and individual customers. In the year 2000, the additional charge and responsibilty of the HR function was also handed down to her.

But Kalpana, who had more or less grown with the brand ICICI, always felt that this model of having a developmental institution separate from a bank was not sustainable. In 2001, she was elevated to the board of ICICI. In some ways that was the pinnacle of everything and on the very same day, she told herself that she had to make the merger work at any cost. The merger was announced in October the same year.

But it was easier thought than done. "We needed to combine the two. You can think of any challenge in the world and it was thrown at us. I knew that was the right thing to do but I don't claim I knew how we were going to do it. We needed to handle regulators, share holders, valuers, investment bankers—it was a massive HR exercise."

In 2001, when the merger was announced internally, there were four companies; a 10,000-strong group of organizations with individually different skill sets and completely different orientation. Obviously, it was the most challenging assignment ever handled by Kalpana. Her leadership was on line in the innumerable calls that she had to take. Nevertheless, she along with her skilled team sailed through effortlessly.

Distress with Dabhol

With the merger behind them, Kalpana was handed over the responsibility of managing the distressed asset portfolio in 2004, while continuing to manage the Bank's corporate centre functions which included planning and strategy, finance, risk management, legal and HR. Whilst Kalpana had been involved with the asset side of the business earlier, she had never headed an asset function. This gave her another opportunity to test 'How do I make it happen!'

"I had committed that by 2006, the department would be dissolved by either selling or restructuring bad assets or turning them around. But I had underestimated the challenge as one of the headline cases in the distressed asset portfolio was Dabhol."

If the merger was a difficult task, the challenge of restructuring Dabhol can be easily rated as more difficult. In Dabhol, with Mr Damodaran who was spearheading the move shifting to the Securities and Exchange Board of India (SEBI), she was suddenly catapulted straight into the eye of the storm.

It was a project over which the Indian government was facing a series of litigations. It exposed Kalpana to not just senior Cabinet ministers and civil servants who were driving it but also the ministries right from power, to petroleum, finance and external affairs. Then there were other stakeholders like NTPC, GAIL, IDBI and SBI on this side. On the US side, there were powerful behemoths like GE and Bectel. The US government was involved because OPIC had lent money and there were some 17 foreign banks involved in addition to the refinance agencies. To top it all, there was Maharashtra government too. Kalpana couldn't have asked for a more potent cocktail for a distressed asset.

"But all is well that ends well. The good news is that by 2006, ICICI had dismantled the distressed asset function. This also included getting Dabhol out of the distressed asset list of ICICI."

Dusk to a New Dawn

The average age of the employees at ICICI is 28. So it was Kalpana's initiative while donning the HR hat, to hold the retirement age at 58. Six months before May 2007, when Kalpana attained her retirement age, she started evaluating an opportunity to undertake a full-scale second career in an executive capacity with an investment bank.

That was the time when ICICI was struggling with bringing in some innovation into raising further capital for the insurance business. In one of the brainstorming sessions, it was mooted that ICICI could create an intermediate company to put in capital and Kalpana was asked to join the company.

"Here was an opportunity to maintain the association with the group that had actually become like a surname for me. I would have lost my surname a bit in moving on to some other company, so I decided to take the offer for the next five years."

It was also a natural progression. However, to date, her biggest achievement has been the returns on her investment in mentoring. "We have a group executive council that has representatives from across all businesses that carry the ICICI name—life insurance, general asset management, private equity, securities and the bank. There are 14 members there barring Mr Kamath and me. Ten out of those 14 are personally mentored by me. It is the greatest pleasure to see them flourish and each one of them has the calibre to head an MNC as a CEO."

The lady attaches great importance to nurturing her team members. She passionately believes that a good leader is not merely someone who can direct the teams in functional areas but also needs to establish a direct emotional connect with people. Given intense work pressures, employees spend most of their time in the work environment away from their families. Thus, bosses and senior colleagues need to be sensitive towards the personal needs and challenges of their employees. To her delight, Kalpana has ended up advising her colleagues in areas as diverse as marriage, starting a family, buying a house and much more, and this has brought her close to others beyond the call of the profession.

Of Cricket and 5000 Runs

Within ICICI, there is a story that stems from a small skit that the ICICI team had put together and was enacted at a party thrown by one of the seniors. The junior colleagues got together to enact the play, acting as the senior members of the team. The set was a table where most of the top echelons of ICICI were pondering over a new win from the Board of Cricket Control of India (BCCI), where the board had outsourced the selection of the Indian cricket team to ICICI. The company was to decide on the charter of the team and then go on to select the players accordingly.

Doing a fantastic job of mimicking Kalpana's mannerism and style, the junior said that ICICI needed to start by setting a goal for the team. So she proposed, they set a goal of 5000 runs for test matches! The others in the room reacted saying it was a rather steep target to fix. In any case, fixing such a target would require changing the rule book of the game.

However, Kalpana's acting clone in her characteristic way, found a way around the arguments and convinced the panel that the target should be 5000 and rest all could be managed.

Though the skit was supposed to be a pun on Kalpana's perseverance and in some ways, her being a hard task master, difficult to convince, Kalpana has used the '5000-run' story as a bouncer.

"After that day, each time my team came up and said achieving some targets were impossible, I would quote the 5000 run story."

Woman What?

To a great extent, she has been a lady with luck on her side with mentors giving her a lot of space and opportunity to grow. She flourished with seniors who were ready to risk a lot by putting their bets on her capabilities.

"It is rather odd to say I was reporting to people like Mr Kamath or Mr Vaghul as they were more of people influencers...they opened your eyes to the various possibilities and then left you to it...if you had a problem, you could go back to them. I would have hated bosses who'd peep down my shoulder to see what I was doing and then would have wanted to second guess me on what I ought to have done."

In fact, during her entire stint with ICICI, Kalpana does not remember a single day when she felt she was on the wrong side of the gender.

"Even today why women do so well at ICICI is due to the fact that it is a merit-based organization. I never got an assignment or was never denied a promotion because of my gender. Or for that matter, there was never a difference in emoluments as compared to my male colleagues. Diversity always thrives in an organization that is merit based. And the acceptance by the male colleagues has to be cent per cent."

"When I joined, there were very few women. So effectively, I grew up in ICICI, bonding a lot with my male colleagues and I have no reason to complain."

"My closest female friendships within ICICI started only in the mid-90s when Shikha Sharma (CEO of Life Insurance), Renuka Ramnath (CEO of ICICI Venture), Ramni Nirula (Senior General Manager at ICICI Bank) and I would sometimes form the 'girls club' and holiday or party together."

Woman who Conquered Adversity

Life's biggest strength comes from conquering adversities. As one copes with adversities, there is an explosion of strength and one has to know the art of channelizing it into accomplishing the impossible. Kalpana's biggest setback as a woman came from the fact that she could not become a mother.

"Despite all the doomcasters in my younger days in school and college, I sailed past beautifully, year after year. There were no failures. But, the fact that I couldn't have children and as a woman, I had yearned to become a mother, was a big setback that took time and a lot of effort to handle."

To Kalpana, that was the biggest disability that a woman could face. "But it makes you much stronger and pushes you to say: 'now let me go out and do the impossible'. You want to prove to yourself that you can do it. When I told myself that I have got to get the merger done, if you ask me, did I know how to do it? No, I did not. But I knew that I had to get it done and figure out a way to do it. Adversities can give you the ultimate sense of purpose. I think it's the theory of constraints."

Today Kalpana is a complete woman. At the first public recognition that she got from the Indian Merchant Chambers Women's Wing in Mumbai, Kalpana walked up to the podium and proved it.

"There are several people that you can thank when you get an award. I can thank many of my mentors but

Accepting an award from Prime Minister Manmohan Singh

I am not going to do that. If you ask me, I stand here to really celebrate India's womanhood because if I was born a 100 years ago, I would have been thrown out of my house or would have suffered the ignominy of my husband bringing a second wife home who would bear him a child and a son at that. Instead, I am standing in front of you with my achievements being honoured.

"That is what freedom means to me as a woman living in the new look India: My life is an ode to Indian womanhood where it doesn't matter whether a woman is married or not or is a mother or not. She is an individual in her own right."

Kalpana also went on to win the business woman leader awards from *Economic Times* and Zee. In 2006, she made it to the *Forbes* list of 100 most-powerful women in the world.

Up Close and Personal

On the personal front, Kalpana moved out of the joint family before she joined ICICI. Since she does not have any children, she did not have to make any trade-offs in terms of time spent with family that many of her other colleagues would have had to cope with. Jai keeps busy with his business of neon signs and plastic boards and has never been resentful of the time that Kalpana has given to her work. Theirs is a large 60-member extended family and it becomes quite a task when all of them get together.

In her many years in corporate life, Kalpana may have metamorphosed quite a bit but the basics remain unchanged—her love for Bollywood and of course, her love for dressing up. Shopping for jewellery and clothes is still a favourite pastime. She can never leave a city she visits without stealing that half an hour to shop.

"I wear all sorts of clothes. Saris are the corporate attire in India but when I travel abroad, I have a full western wardrobe. Weekends are for casual wear and *salwar kameez*...so I maintain three wardrobes."

The Way Forward

Kalpana admits that all the concepts of retirement were shaped in an era when life expectancy was 60-65. Now the same is moving to 75 and even early 80s. The active period of an average person is getting extended. However, the paradox is that we have a very young population so we cannot do much with the retirement age. No wonder there are an increasing number of people who are now pursuing a second career.

"Post retirement, one can easily get a 12-year shot at a second career. If I had taken a break from ICICI and taken up a second career, that's how I would have managed it. This is the time to transition from executive to an advisory role but it is still full time. Between 63 and 70, I would still be active in the corporate world, but not necessarily on a full-time basis."

Even at 58, Kalpana is on a journey of self-discovery and learning is an unending process. Given the singular focus that Kalpana's mother had on house work, the kids never dabbled with any sport like swimming, cycling or horse riding. But for Kalpana it is never too late. She has taken to working out four times a week for the past eight years and is also trying her hands at swimming. And then there is always the urge to tee off.

But with age, there is another side of Kalpana that is itching to get involved in improving lives not just by cutting cheques but by contributing her time and energy.

"Until some months ago, my social contribution was writing out cheques but I feel, I have been very selfish and I need to give personal time too. We have set up the ICICI Foundation for Inclusive Growth in which I am involved. With my family, I am also setting up a school in Gujarat in the memory of my mother."

For Kalpana, however, the biggest take-away from her own story is the fact that every child has a spark. But in her case, it took her ages to really unleash the pent-up desire to lead from the front. And it happened only when she stepped into ICICI and got the environment that was conducive for her aspirations to take wings. Now that she looks back with baby eyes, she recognizes that the biggest force that can actually ignite the imagination of children is teachers. They have the power to help tiny hands touch the stars or fall flat on the ground.

Kalpana reminisces a setback at school in 1965, the antidote for which, however, she got only in the 80s after she joined ICICI.

"At Walsingham, it was a day when I had to walk up to the podium and speak out the thought for the day. The stage fright caught on me and I fumbled miserably. My English teacher, who was something of a terror, nearly battered me in front of the whole class as if I had committed a heinous crime. It shattered my confidence to no end."

It was only in the 80s when ICICI sent her to talk at the RBI's Bankers Training College that she geared herself up to conquer this fear. "I spoke there and the Principal called up my head of department to say that I had acted as a veteran batsmen, fielding all the balls with great finesse. It's this certification that restored my damaged confidence as far as public speaking is concerned. But it took years to repair the bruised spirit!"

These are the reasons why I feel the need to look at education not just in the form of sporadic things like building schools. All that will happen of its own steam. I want to invest time and effort in training teachers. A couple of decades ago, teaching was a noble profession but we have not invested enough as a nation to scale it up. We need to roll up our sleeves to give them their due and give this nation a sparkling future in its children."

A look at her corporate score card and the success rate of her mentoring skills and one would know that Kalpana will figure out how to make it happen!

* * * * *

Kalpana feels: "My life is an ode to Indian womanhood where it doesn't matter whether a woman is married or not or is a mother or not. She is an individual in her own right"

In 2007, Naina was awarded the *Padma Shri* by the then President APJ Abdul Kalam for her exemplary work in the field of Trade and Industry

THREE

Glass Ceilings are in the Mind

Naina Lal Kidwai

CEO, HSBC

Naina was a child of strange contradiction. On one hand she swore by convention. As a result, life was all about being straight and guarded. There was a preamble to follow, and the rule book was never to be defied. On the other hand, she was a questioning individual. To her, everything was born out of reason and if the reason was not in the near vicinity of her tiny self, there was need for some serious probing.

Born on 16 April 1957, Naina's early years were governed by the abridged rule book with simple dos and don'ts, handed down to her through generations. It had typical axioms like 'good girls always stood first in their class', and many more. Therefore, Naina's uneasiness as a runner-up was quite obvious when someone else walked away with the topper's trophy. That was the year when Naina's grandfather had passed away and she missed her school for three months. The defeat broke her tiny but aggressively competitive heart. Hurt and aided by limited understanding of life's complications, Naina was not ready to forgive her parents for keeping her away from school and thus bringing upon her the first defeat.

Naina's parents were well-meaning individuals. They neither brushed aside their daughter's somewhat rigid childhood regime nor did they get overtly paranoid about it. They were instrumental in moulding her personality. Her father Surendr Lal (better known as Bandy Lal) had long chats with her regarding the importance of winning and taught her to learn from her mistakes. As a result, Naina grew up more tolerant towards the vagaries of life—of success and failure.

Dinner-Table Conversations

Naina was born in Kolkata but her early education took place in Mumbai where her father was posted. Naina and her sister received much of their practical education over the dining table. Dinner was an important event of the day and the family made it a point to dine together.

"Now that I look back, I realize that the seeds of what my sister and I have accomplished in life were sown in the formative years during the long discussions that we used to have on the dining table. My dad was in the insurance business and was an avid golfer. I seem to have picked up the knack for finances from him while my sister took after his love for the game."

Naina's most-cherished outings were her visits to her father's office. On days when their father worked late, Naina's mother Prem Mohini Lal would send the two sisters to get him from office after finishing their dinner so that they could see him before going to bed.

Those short visits were great fun as he would be expecting his daughters and would keep chocolates that they would devour with great delight. Going to the office also meant opening the drawers and looking at the neatly piled-up stuff—documents, pencils, erasers, note books. He was very methodical and the way he kept his things would inspire organized work habits in any workplace. The influence of that corporate ambience stayed etched in their minds forever.

Naina's sister Nonita Lal Qureshi, a leading golfer and winner of the Arjuna Award in 1989, came to make a living from her father's first love, that is, golf. Mr Lal prepared the memorandum of understanding and started the Professional Golfers Association. His daughter followed his footsteps by participating in setting up many golf institutions across the country.

"This encourages me to believe that childhood influences are quite important and have a strong impression in our lives and also go on to assist us in becoming what we finally make of ourselves. Mom was a proud homemaker who maintained a beautiful house. I still have a very guilty feeling if the napkins are not placed right on the dining table or if anything is amiss. Her influence has remained with me till date. She was a very strong woman and spent a lot of time helping people and doing social work. That is what my sister and I have carried on."

Ms Sombre and Studious

As a child, Naina was very hard working. "Compared to what I was, my daughter Kemaya is quite different. She is bright, rather brighter than I ever was. She gets by with very little work. This really distresses me because I feel she can always put a little more effort and do much better than I ever did. But I guess she's more balanced in certain ways and is living a life that is more fun."

But that's the take of the mother in Naina. As a teenager, she was different. She was shy and that is probably the reason that made her a voracious reader. Her most-cherished moments were the hours that she used to spend with the written word.

"I remember as a kid when my parents had friends over. I would lock myself in the washroom just to finish the book and avoid doing rounds of the customary hellos and *namastes*!"

Naina's mother was not very happy seeing her daughter dither away from house chores.

"I was clumsy at handling chores and that confirmed that I was meant for things beyond house-keeping and it was safe for both me and the family crockery that I stuck to my books and things that I enjoyed doing."

At eleven, Naina went to study at a boarding school. She landed at Tara Hill—a Loreto Convent boarding school in Shimla. For the first time in life she was away from her parents. Moving beyond the riding and tennis classes that she partook in Mumbai, she explored new extracurricular activities. And this time there were no limitations due to school, or the lack of space that she had grown up with in their somewhat-small Mumbai house.

Suddenly, Naina who had never before played team games found herself excelling in basketball and throw ball. It was a fabulous experience for her to become a part of the school team by the end of her first year. Naina and her two friends stayed in the school basketball team from grade 8 to 11. She also went on to play at the state level for Himachal Pradesh.

"The game instilled in me a serious sense of purpose, discipline, loyalty and team-play. There was no one star, it was team spirit all through. I used to play the middle and the back, so I was not the one who got to shoot goals. But I had learnt early in life that you don't always have to be the one who wins accolades."

In bitter cold, spring and through fall, the team would get up before sunrise and practice because they were the leading team in the city and wanted to stay that way. "For the first time, I realized that gaining leadership position was one thing, but maintaining it needed sweat and blood."

Boarding school also honed Naina's sensitivities towards other things in life from which she had kept herself away for long. She started taking piano lessons and her deep interest in western classical music took off. And from this urge to create good music by working in tandem with an orchestra, she picked up her first few lessons in taking everyone along in management—the skill that was to come real handy in later life.

She also started dabbling with theatrics. Coming from a girls' convent where boys were not allowed, and thanks to her tall frame and rough voice, Naina inevitably landed up playing the men's role in school plays. In the school opera, she played the lovelorn Ralph

Rackstraw in *Daddy Long Legs*. She participated in elocution and debate competitions which groomed her for public speaking which later proved most beneficial for her business.

She had a wonderful piano teacher who gave her double promotions through various years of learning. So she was at a level which was beginning to require a lot of hard work. There were different aspects to her personality that started to surface. The 'studying hard and being a good girl' streak remained, but team-play and music went a long way in rounding up her personality.

Naina went on to become the school headgirl, house-captain, library-squad captain and all this taught her the values of fairness, justice and transparency which has stood her in good stead through life.

Eye of the Mind

The years at Loreto also made Naina look at spirituality in a new light. Being a convent, there was a guided exposure to religion, but the good thing was that Christianity was not thrust down their throats.

They were quite disciplined in going to the Chapel once a week and the chapel service also played Hindu hymns. It had messages with lots of moral education.

This was not Naina's first exposure to spiritualism. Coming from a staunch Hindu background, she had always joined her mother and grandmother in the puja room to put the *chandan* or to sit through the *bhajans*. But back then, the motivational factors were different.

"I always had the eye on the *prasad* and the goodies that the kids would get at the end of the rituals."

School however, introduced her to intellectual spiritualism vis-à-vis the rituals of religion at home. Frankly, it could be because things were taught in English and understanding and assimilating a deep thought did not mean understanding Sanskrit *shlokas*."

Tell Me Why?

Even at 17, Naina's habit of questioning all and sundry had not subsided. Exposure to science in school had only fuelled her quest to find the underlying cause of everything around her. Armed with the newfound confidence of a teenager, that year Nina questioned the purpose of her mother's regular trips to an *ashram* in the Himalayas. Her mother would go and stay there for months together and this prompted Naina to question her mother for leaving the family and going away for such long periods.

Her father acted the moderator. He sat with Naina and told her that it was good to question but not without knowing the absolute truth. Half-baked truths could be dangerous and misleading. She was told that one has to learn to live with others without always dictating ones own terms and conditions. So, Naina decided to make the trip with her mother to see what was it that her mother was seeking from those visits to the *ashram*.

"I stayed there with my mother for a month and followed the rigorous schedule of getting up early in the morning, cleaning the place, participating in the cooking and listening to the sermons on Hinduism."

That was to be another turning point in her life. She had heard stories about all the unexplainable experiences that people had had at the *ashram*. But she was soon to witness one of them and quick to learn not to question what could not be explained.

"I vividly remember the evening when we were sitting under the pipal tree with the sound of the leaves rustling in the evening breeze. Suddenly, these white lights started descending from the hill across and travelling down to the river bed." She brushed them aside as people with lanterns or vehicles with headlights driving down some hill road. The *ashram* residents, however, insisted they were celestial lights.

The rationalist in Naina thought she would prove her point. So the next morning she went to investigate only to discover a bare cliff without any motorable roads that would have made it impossible for any human form with a lantern or a light to walk straight down at the speed at which the lights had descended. She still does not know where the lights came from or what they were—some scientific phenomenon or a divine one—but she certainly learned to respect what one does not understand.

It taught Naina to develop a tolerance for questions that still beg an answer or for faiths that people live by. She went on to marry a Muslim and this understanding and tolerance helped her to bring up a family that was equally tolerant towards all faiths and religions and all schools of thought.

Delhi Stint

College was an easy decision. By then, Naina's parents had moved to Delhi and she was ready to come back and spend some time with them. She joined Lady Shriram College to pursue Economics (Hons).

"Times have changed. Unlike today when parents are very involved in their kids' education, I don't remember my parents getting as involved with where I was joining and what I should pursue. We sort of discussed and I filled up the form, stood in the line and went for the interview. Now-a-days, it's like livewire and both parents and students are stressed out over getting into the right college."

College was another learning experience for Naina. She, of course, was more easily distracted now in a new city with quite a few pursuits on her platter and newer influences. However, the leadership strain remained intact. In the first year at college, she stood for the College Union Secretary position and got elected by the students. She went on to become the President of the college students' union. In fact, Vinita Bali, now managing director of Britannia, who was two years her senior in college, egged her on to give it a try.

"I thought it was suicidal as I didn't have the support base and most students who come to college in Delhi have friends from school while I had come from a smaller school in Shimla. But she encouraged me to take the plunge and so I did."

During her years as president, LSR had their first-ever college festival. They went around collecting funds, getting trophies instituted and most important of all, breaking away from the convention of not having boys participate in the festival.

But outside of college, Naina remained the nice and serious girl who would ride the auto-rickshaws with scissors hidden behind her. After all, Delhi was not a very safe place to be. "I would always travel with a pair of scissors but now that I look back, I do not know how that would have helped if the auto-rickshaw driver acted funny. What could I have done (chopped his hair perhaps)? But at that time it gave me great comfort to have it on me."

Reluctant Chartered Accountant

The choice of economics had left open a number of fields for Naina to pursue. At the same time, there weren't many women in finance. It was defying convention and she did not feel very comfortable with the initial thought. Naina's father pushed her to take up accountancy. Instead, Naina wanted to pursue Masters in business, abroad.

"I do not know how that got into my head as I didn't know a soul who had pursued an MBA in the US. The only possible influence would be that of my friend Mira Nair who was studying at Harvard. We used to talk regularly and maybe that was what had made me realize that there was a life worth exploring on the other side of the ocean."

But to enroll in a business school, it was mandatory for her to be 19 years old and also required some experience. So her father egged her to take up CA in the meanwhile and committed that she could study MBA abroad provided she got a berth in one of the top five business schools. So CA is what she set out to do. She wanted to go with a global name so PricewaterhouseCoopers is what she set her mind and heart on.

Naina applied and walked into the interview only to be told the same old, oft-repeated story: she had all the credentials but the company was not ready to hire a woman! What would they possibly do with her? She would be the only woman and the job entailed travelling to dacoit-infested places to audit companies. Naina returned home quite disappointed.

Well, do with me what you do with the others, she told them. "I tried to reason it out and told them that there always has to be a first time and maybe other women hadn't been along. But they had a hundred and one reasons why women could not join the profession."

She did not hear from them for a month-and-a-half at which point she decided to crack-up on her father. He was a man of high principals and never asked for favours. He never used his position for his selfish interests. But Naina made him call up PWC and find out what had happened and if there was any chance of reconsideration. With that little push and influence, she finally got a call. There obviously were other women applicants and three of them were appointed for the first time that year.

The same head of the Delhi office who went on to become a friend and also became the Country Head for PWC India, told Naina ten years later that the company is actively discriminating against women to keep them out of the cadre in order to maintain a 50:50 ratio within the organization. In the absence of this policy, the fairer sex could very well cross the 70 per cent mark, given the calibre of women who apply today.

"So it just goes to show how quickly things can change and how just for the lack of imagination on the part of organizations and the male-centricity, women were being kept out. I do not know how many women were turned away by then. Had I accepted the diktat, I would have ended up with some middle-sized accounting firm where I would have learned something but it would not have given me the exposure, confidence and the comfort level that I was to earn during my time with PWC."

It was a great learning experience as she had to go to audit for a number of companies. She went on to join Grindlays later but her relationship with the bank began with an audit that she undertook for them. She audited SBI and got the opportunity to understand the working of a domestic bank vis-à-vis a multinational one.

They also had their share of fun. They used to 'car-pool' for the audits. Seven or eight of us would jump into a car and drive off to places like Faridabad or Ballabhgarh. "It was great fun but it also meant a lot of hard work. I dreaded the day it was my car-pool day as it meant driving through the dusty and unfriendly roads in and around Delhi and the adjoining areas.

That is where my networking within the finance fraternity started. During those years, I made friends who I am still in touch with. While the work and the degree course in itself were terribly boring, they were very enriching in terms of companies that one got to know and people that one got to work with."

Business Beckoned

All this while, Naina kept filling up forms to apply to Harvard and Wharton. Those were the days of manual typewriters and it took her some effort to fill in the forms. And unlike today there were no consultants telling you what the business schools wanted to hear. So she was at it all alone, not knowing what it takes to get to the coveted institution. Moreover, she was under

Naina wears only cotton and silk handloom that symbolizes the rich tradition of the weavers

pressure because her parents would let her go only if she got into one of the best schools.

Her efforts paid and unexpectedly so, she got into Harvard and Wharton even before she finished her accountancy. Naina wrote back to them to see if they were ready for delayed joining. But they were not interested in blocking the seats. Unlike today, those days there was a rule in the Chartered Accounting programme, wherein one could not take final examination till training was finished. So Naina took the plunge and decided to come back for her accountancy examination at a later date.

View from the West

All of 23, Naina had the most exciting opportunities awaiting her. But her parents were concerned. There were no precedents to follow. She was the first Indian woman to get into Harvard. Her mother was not sure if she could trust the West with her daughter. So it took a bit of convincing by her daughter that she would not stray and would stick to her value system. That taken care of, Naina packed for her first visit to the USA, landing straight into the rigorous schedule of Harvard.

"I had never been to the States before. I had travelled Europe earlier with a friend on a Eurorail pass and that was the only exposure that I had to a foreign country."

So Naina began by learning how to use an ATM and shop at the supermarket. She had never visited a superstore earlier and was clueless about selecting a particular jam out of the hundred brands on the rack, stacked one against another. At this point, the study group that

Harvard traditionally forms came to her rescue. Those in her group gave her the first few orientation lessons and taught her how to select the best and the cheapest. They explained what private labels are and this helped Naina in settling in.

Naina was also the youngest in her class. Other Indians were practically in their 30s—IIT graduates who had come to US to work and were doing their MBAs. They took Naina under their wings and she got her supply of *desi* food regularly.

With this, Naina stepped into a different world and the rest became history. They had great teachers and she had the opportunity to work under Michael Potter who was the guru of Competitive Strategies. She did her seminar under Potter as well and did a consulting assignment under him for which she was to get two credits.

"I learned a lot about strategy and competitive behaviour which was very interesting. We learned right through the MBA course on how information can be distilled from reams of data thrown at you and how that can be analysed and communicated effectively. You had to speak in class and you got rated for it. It was not easy because the Americans sometimes speak even before they think. We Indians usually deliberate before saying anything so it was a challenge to be heard in a crowd of some 80-odd bright people."

The other challenge was somewhat predictable. Unlike today when women constitute almost one-third of the gender mix, in those days there were just 17 women in a class of 80. Only two of them were from Asia.

Harvard was ready for diversity but Indian parents were not yet ready to explore and let the capabilities of their daughters grow!

"My being the first woman from India at HBS was less a statement of capability because I am sure there were other women who could have done it before me. It was an indication of the lack of social support and awareness."

And then came the campus recruitment phase and Naina found herself swayed by the temptation to stay back and make a career in the US. The companies came wooing and she was interviewed for a position in Manhattan and New York. She loved the thought of working there.

But Naina had left India with a clear vision of returning home. She spoke to all the people she knew in India who suggested that if her final intention was to return, then a couple of years of experience abroad would not hold much store back home. Indian banking landscape was getting competitive and it was the right time to start her career. Naina was interviewed by Citibank and told them she wanted a job in India. She got the job but on her way back stopped by at London to attend an interview with Grindlays Bank. She bagged that job too.

Homecoming

Back home, Naina spoke with the industry and decided to join Grindlays because it was the largest foreign bank and had an investment banking operation in India, which she was permitted to join directly. The bank did not insist upon the two years induction programme that was compulsory for others.

For the next four years, Naina dabbled with investment banking and finally moved on to head the Mumbai operations of Grindlays, which was a great step for the bank and for her. Later she asked to be moved to Delhi which was very unusual because Delhi was not a big business hub for Grindlays at that time. However, Naina had personal reasons for being in the capital. She had been away for long and wanted to be with her parents. Also the smaller operation would give Naina a lot of flexibility to perform. During her tenure, Delhi did become the largest investment operation for Grindlays. That was a fulfilling time for Naina and became her launch pad to bigger avenues. In 1989, she took over as the head of the investment banking operation for the bank.

"That was path-breaking in an organization that had no women in senior positions and that favoured age and seniority. My predecessor was typically grey-haired and had at least 15 years or more of work experience. So I had to keep pushing the envelope not so much in terms of gender as in terms of age. Fortunately for me, the organization was also evolving into meritocracy and the timing was right."

Time to Tango

Naina was 33 and had been heading the investment banking operations for Grindlays for sometime now. But there had neither been time nor the compulsion to marry so far. Then the unexpected happened. Naina found herself accepting the friendship of Rishid Kidwai—a man who absolutely matched her idea of an ideal life-partner.

"I think he recognized and accepted that here was a woman who was completely focused and a little pig-headed about her career. But he was comfortable in his own skin and had no problems accepting me for what I was. He indeed encouraged me."

Naina was comfortable about marrying a Muslim and her parents loved Rishid and were elated with her decision of marrying at all. But there were issues to be tackled.

"I was counselled by both parents. They wanted me to understand completely what I was getting into. 'Have you thought through it. We have no problems with the guy but religion is something that you have to think through. What faith would you bring your children up in...' My father had many Muslim friends and we had a very open house. But my parents also took some time to accept the match. There were still some senior members in my staunch Hindu family who thought I had committed a horrific act. But it was long since I had started taking rule books less seriously."

However, from Rishid's side, the family was very progressive. Many of his cousins were married outside the community.

"We had our ideological fights and one that took a long time to resolve was my not taking his family name. I was Naina Lal and he was Rishid Kidwai. I remember we would meet people, who did not know us very well, at parties and they would think we were living in sin since I didn't carry his family name to prove we were married. It was only after Kamaya was born that I finally softened my stance of switching over to Naina Lal Kidwai."

Naina evolved and realized that it would have been difficult for her daughter to handle the relationship if her mother did not show complete acceptance of belonging to one family.

"The story with Rishid is different. To this day, he objects to being called Mr Naina Lal and some invitations that are thus addressed have to be hidden before he sees them. I don't mind being called Mrs Rishid Kidwai but he has a problem with Mr Naina Lal! But those are our sweet pain points. He remains my friend, my severest critic, and my support. He is the guy who keeps me rooted to the ground, my reality check."

As a businesswoman, she was fortunate to have a husband from the business world who had worked 30 years with the corporate sector and understood the language of business. He was able to advise her much better on office politics as he understood the nuances in depth.

However, it was not just Rishid who helped Naina through. Naina was very fortunate to marry into an enlightened family. In fact, Rishid's grandfather Shaikh Abdullah started the Muslim women's education movement in Aligarh. He went on to start the Women's College which is now part of the Aligarh Muslim University. He literally had to bodily protect the first group of women students who joined the college in an era where conservative Muslims would attempt to remove the purdah of the *palkis* in which the girls would travel, in order to discourage them from attending classes.

In addition, her mother-in-law Birjees Kidwai was a blessing in disguise, thanks to her never-ending support. During the time when both Naina and Rishid had their jobs and had to travel at the same time, she would seek help from her mother-in-law who would fly to Mumbai and baby-sit Kamaya. Naina also learned lessons in generosity and caring for others from her mother-in-law.

"It wasn't easy for her to fly at one week's notice but she would do it. My mother hated travelling but my sister was also a great help around those difficult times."

The Professional Itch

And then the bank put its hand in the Pandora's Box. Naina had been at investment banking for almost four years. In good faith, the bank had started talking to her about her next move since they thought that she was ready for some additional responsibility within the bank. The most logical progression was corporate banking but Naina did not think it challenging enough. At that point in time, corporate banking would mean selling name-loan to the likes of Tatas and Mahindras. It was not at all financially challenging.

"I wanted to do retail banking and told them that. They nearly dropped off their chairs. Retail banking had a much older fraternity and the management exposure was rather huge. They tried to dissuade me but it didn't seem to be working."

Destiny's Bouncer

One morning, Bob Edgar, the then CEO of the bank called Naina into his office and popped an offer. He wanted Naina to start the NRI global service for the retail wing of the bank that had by now become ANZ Grindlays. It meant tremendous opportunity and was a role where Naina was expected to open new NRI centres all over the world.

To Bob's surprise, Naina did not jump with joy at the offer. She did not thank him saying that's what she had wanted to do all her life. All she said was that she would think about it and get back to him. She left a confused Bob to discuss the issue with Rishid.

Naina had been aggressively clamouring for the next success in life, but destiny had bestowed her with a bigger gift. A couple of days before Bob made the offer, she had been told that she was expecting her first baby.

"The bank was putting faith in me and I did not know whether I would live up to the expectations. I had no idea what being pregnant was like at that point in time. There was fear of the unknown. I went home and spoke about it at length with Rishid. We decided, I should go back the next day and confide in Bob."

Next day the mother-to-be shared the news with Bob. There was a stunned silence that descended on his face. She was very uncomfortable and quite sure he would say that the bank would think about it and get back to her. But he didn't. Instead he asked, if Naina was comfortable accepting the job.

"I wanted to give it a try. I had no idea whether I would lay flat on my back. I did not know and had no way of knowing how fitful or smooth my pregnancy would be but I intended to work till my way to the hospital."

Bob looked Naina in the eye and said, "The job is yours if you want it."

As they say, the will to health and to happiness lies within and not outside of self. The faith that the bank put in her cemented her resolve to succeed. She was now determined to prove that the bank had not erred in

After she has had her fill of corporate life, Naina is inclined to join what has almost become the 'Kidwai tradition' of making life better for the women folk, through education and by creating means of employment

putting it's faith in her. She worked till the last minute, from the hospital bed, and was back in office within six weeks of delivering Kamaya.

In fact, Naina's boss and Rishid were the ones to get jitters at the attitude of this go-getter mother who did not cease from travelling even in her eighth month. On the day Rajiv Gandhi was assassinated, Naina had her bags packed to leave for a training programme in Dubai. Her team of 45 managers from across the Middle East was in Dubai and Naina who was the leader was to get there with the training material along with another colleague. As Rishid drove to see her off at the airport, they sensed tension in the air. They were stopped on the Mumbai roads and asked to head back home as no one was sure about the turn of events after the assassination.

She was not turning back for anything and reached the airport but Rishid still teases her about how she was so obsessed with getting onboard the plane that she never bothered about how he was going to get home safe.

Around the same time, the plane in which Bob was travelling experienced a forced landing. He was left thinking what would have happened if it was Naina facing that forced landing in the eighth month of her pregnancy. He stopped sanctioning any more travel for her and Naina lost the battle of wits to her husband and her boss.

However, Kamaya's birth turned out to be a bigger and more tasking event for the workaholic mother. She had to balance her motherhood with the ambitious calling that she had chosen to pursue. But to this day, Kamaya and her family remain her greatest joy. The family was now complete with the daughter and her step-son Rumaan who had lived with them since he was nine. The family now consists of an older child who is very mature and creative at 27 and Kamaya who is 15 and great fun.

"Not having another child was a conscious decision that we took as a family—partly due to my career and also because we didn't want to create two against one to give Rumaan his due as our son. That has worked quite nicely."

Lady Luck

The kids brought pots full of luck for Naina professionally as well. As the Gulf war broke out, new vistas of opportunity opened up in Naina's line of business—the NRI services for ANZ Grindlays. All the Indian money in the Gulf began to flow back into India. The contribution of the business went up to 60 per cent of ANZ Grindlays' deposits. And she found herself centrestage at the best part of the show with the most focused audience.

Success is more or less situational. She earned her laurels very easily, thanks to the circumstances and they came in areas where people were very skeptical to have her in the first place. That made way for her to go on and head the retail operations for the bank in western India. It meant dropping straight into the midst of worker unions and managing 2,500 people. It taught her to manage large teams and that was a very important learning.

In 1994, India began to open up and the world of investment banking started taking keen interest in the Indian market. She got feelers from time to time but was not tempted to exit Grindlays. She was sitting on top of retail banking and the path that would have led her to becoming the CEO was not clear. Some held the view that she should take a foreign stint but like earlier times, she was reluctant to go and live abroad. She found herself at crossroads.

Once again Naina felt that she seemed to have outrun age in reaching certain milestones in life. She was young and CEOs those days were expected to be more senior, experienced and grey-haired candidates. So she had to wait and do something else in the meantime.

The head hunters had been making lucrative offers. Finally, Morgan Stanley gained her favour because that gave her the opportunity to start their investment banking in India from scratch.

"I loved Grindlays. I had been there for 13 years and I literally had to tear myself apart from the organization. The only thing that was an issue to my mind was the differential pay scale between foreigners and Indians that the bank used to offer. I was as well educated, as efficient if not better, than my foreign peers but there was a disparate salary structure. The only condition that made Morgan Stanley clinch the deal was that I would be paid as much as comparable foreign employees in my position. It was a matter of principal."

Naina joined Morgan Stanley and the media went berserk with reports of her becoming the highest paid woman executive in India. But not just as a woman, she was possibly one of the highest paid professionals in India at that time. This was followed by about eight years of investment banking and great fun.

While at Morgan Stanley, she had her first interaction with Nimesh Kampani that was to lead her company into a joint venture with JM Financial. Morgan Stanley was a small team of 10-12 people with a number of people flying in from abroad in order to help Indian operations. She took kludges and persuaded the company to hire locally.

"The guys I hired at that time went on to head Morgan Stanley's operations in Asia—one went on to head equity capital markets and other to head M&A. Once they joined, nobody could have enough of them. We actually opened up a whole new avenue through our Indian office for recruiting Indian professionals for our offshore network."

But Indian markets being what they were in the 1990s, attempting business in India was not easy. It was all about fighting for attention. India was not centre-stage and it meant fighting for space. Much effort went into positioning the country to begin with. It was also difficult to attract money and support from the parent company when they could go and work in other attractive hot markets that were easier to enter like China.

"I remember the time when we got prospective investors to meet Yashwant Sinha, P Chidambaram and every one in the corridors of power to sell India to investors who are now coming in hordes. There were immense problems. The market was not one of the best, the way it is today. We had physical stocks—vaults full of certificates. We did not have a depository and had the Bombay Stock Exchange but no National Stock Exchange."

That was the time when Indian markets were in their infancy. She sat on a number of committees and groups that were instituted to study and add value to the Indian stock exchange and trading systems. "It was certainly an exciting time where I sat with Hemendra Kothari and Nimesh Kampani in teams that would deliberate and help set up the architecture for the Indian markets." She was a part of the team that deliberated the need for the National Stock Exchange. They tried convincing BSE to change but transition to the modern way of thinking seemed impossible for India's oldest stock exchange.

"That experience of being in India was very gratifying. The advantage though was that being with Morgan Stanley, I could access the best practices across the world and position it with the committee that was calling for information from offshore sources."

Finally things started moving. The national depository had taken off. These were the formative days when the Securities and Exchange Board of India (SEBI) had just been set up and GV Ramakrishna, Chairman, SEBI relied on the team that had Naina in it, to set up a self-regulatory association of merchant bankers.

Within Morgan Stanley, once the joint venture was formed, she asked for relocation to Delhi. Privatization was getting mainstream and with most clients being in Delhi, she was spending half her week in Delhi. She thought it would be easier for her to live in Delhi and keep travelling to Mumbai. That was the time she was working on domestic listing for Maruti and also Wipro in Bangalore for their listing with the New York Stock Exchange.

As the next logical step, there were openings in Morgan Stanley abroad but once again she wanted to link her career not with the company but with India. So she made the move to HSBC.

It was an opportunity to head HSBC's Securities and Capital Markets division which dealt with investment banking, equity and capital markets and broking—the businesses that Naina was comfortable handling by then. She joined there with no commitment but an understanding that she would get a shot at moving to the bank in a senior capacity.

"In fact, I had clearly asked what my chances were of becoming the CEO of the bank and they were pretty much clear about the ambition I nursed. But there was no precedent. There had only been one Indian HSBC head in 150 years of the bank's history and no woman ever had headed the bank in any country anywhere in the world. I must have been a bit of a cultural shock for them but I was willing to give it a shot and they were willing to pitch a shot."

Again providence favoured her. The tide was changing and women were being more acceptable in senior positions in world-class institutions. She got the opportunity to become the deputy CEO with HSBC. This with a clear sense that if she delivered as the second in command, she would make it to the top job.

In March 2006, she went on to become the Country Head of HSBC in India with its multiple operations. In October 2006, she became a Group General Manager—one of the top 40 people in the bank globally. In 2007, HSBC group of companies in India employed 32,000 people comprising banking services, insurance, asset management, HSBC Securities & Capital Markets, HSBC Software Development (India) Pvt Ltd and the Global Service Centres (BPO servicing HSBC's operations in the UK, EU and USA).

As the CEO, her activities include running around, meeting people during Townhall meetings that are held on a biannual basis where executives can hear directly from her about the vision and future plans of the bank.

"We are about 32,000 people and India is quite an important hub both business-wise as well as from the point of view of software development and outsourcing. With $14 billion worth of assets being managed by the bank, it has become one of the biggest asset managers in India. We are the market leaders in custody space where 45 per cent of all the Foreign Institutional Investor (FII) money in India is in custody with us."

Success Courts Controversy

Series of successes kissed her feet time and again but for the steel-willed lady, failure and controversies always hovered at the horizon. With each passing day, however, she has become more philosophical about the hits and misses in life.

"Life has been about pushing the envelope. I never take success for granted. And I have learned to take failure in my stride too. For every thing that one achieves, there might be ten others that may not come through. The one thing that I have learned as a woman in the corporate world is to swallow your pride, keep your ego aside and move on. Things that you feel are your well-deserved right, others may feel you don't deserve. They see you either as a woman or different. You just have to learn to walk your way through all the clutter."

Even from her batch from Harvard, only three out of the 17 women have managed to keep their jobs. In the West, it's even more difficult for women to do the balancing act due to lack of help, social support and infrastructure. Negative forces would continue to work around and try to pull one down.

In 2005, Naina was invited on the Board of Nestle SA, the world's largest food company. It was a great honour and a kind of a landmark as she was the first Indian living in India to join the Board of a Fortune 100 company.

But in May 2006, when Naina was elevated to the position of CEO of HSBC, there was some confusion regarding her position as a Board member for Nestle. Interestingly, the lack of precedent added a lot of confusion to the situation. Initially, the regulator stepped in perceiving a conflict of interest. Even though Naina was sure there was no conflict of interest, she had decided to step down from the Nestle SA Board position.

This led to a lot of interest from the media as this was seen, by and large, as a retrograde step for the Indian corporate sector. There was a debate and eventually things fell into place. She continued on the Nestle SA Board while assuming charge as CEO of HSBC Bank along with being Country Head of their Indian operations.

"Now more and more companies abroad want Indians on their boards. And I know it is important for the professionals as well. As an Indian, I am learning a lot by sitting with the Ex-governor of the Bank of England and chairman of Aventis and Vivendi or indeed getting the opportunity to know an outstanding management team at Nestle, led by their charismatic Chairman Peter Brabeck-Letmathe."

Time to Chill

With her job always requiring a lot of travel, Naina would rather stay home and catch up on her sleep on days when she is off work. On working days, she gets an average of three hours of sleep. So there is always a lot of backlog to clear. But when she is not catching up on her sleep, she is holidaying with the family at one of the happening wildlife sanctuaries.

"We have been really lucky in that we sight a tiger every year. They just happen to show up. We like to go and stay in normal boarding that is not a five star. I hate hotels since I have to live so much out of them. We have also done a couple of African safaris that are not as rough as the Indian ones."

At times, the family travels to Gujarat where her husband runs a not-for-profit outfit called the Grassroots Trading Network for Women—a self-empowerment group for women that is promoted by the Self-employed Women's Association (SEWA).

Her hunger for news and being well-informed urges her to read books and magazines on management. In leisure she usually listens to Pundit Hari Prasad Chaurasia, Zakir Hussain or Vilayat Khan.

A few years ago, one would have caught Naina on the wrong foot on her knowledge about Indian cinema. But her son Rumaan has changed things. Though, the influence of long-time friend Mira Nair has always been with her but Indian cinema has become a part of dinner table conversation after Rumaan worked with Mani Ratnam as assistant producer for the Bollywood blockbuster *Guru*. He was also associated with another Bollywood hit *Bunty & Bubli*. Her daughter also worked in Mira Nair's *Monsoon Wedding* when she was nine years old.

"The whole world of Bollywood has become part of family conversation now. Rishid and I are updated about the latest films and gossip. So our horizons are still expanding with newer members of the family opening newer worlds to us."

Sari—the Second Skin

In early days Naina would never be spotted in a *salwar-kameez* or sari. When she became the president of LSR, the principal of the college pointed out that she would be the first president who would be seen around in western outfits. But that was not to change her.

In later life, Naina consciously chose to keep a low profile. The profession in which she was fighting for a foothold needed her to look serious. So the choice of sari as the day-to-day attire was deliberate and used more as a way of telling people that she was a serious-minded person who meant business.

"Not many people know that when I went for my first interview at PricewaterhouseCooper, I was wearing a sari that was pinned up with 25 safety pins! More than what I was saying at the interview, I was concerned about my sari surviving the test."

She consciously decided to adopt the sari also because of her deep love for handloom. She wears only cotton and silk handloom that symbolizes the rich tradition of the weavers. She does occasionally switch to suits for board meetings abroad.

"As far as jewellery is concerned, I never go out buying it. But I enjoy wearing what I have inherited. I love old jewellery—anything that is steeped in Indian tradition."

Future Perfect

The year 2007 saw the *Padma Shri*, one of the highest civilian awards, being bestowed on Naina by the Government of India, for her exemplary work in the field of Trade and Industry.

Before that, she was named in the '50 Women to Watch' report issued by the *Wall Street Journal* in 2006.

With Rishid, Kamaya and Rumaan: When she is not catching up on her sleep, she is holidaying with the family at one of the happening wildlife sanctuaries

She was ranked 34th in the list of world's top 50 businesswomen announced by the *Wall Street Journal* in November 2004. She was ranked 3rd in Asia by *Fortune* magazine in their first ever listing of 'The World's Top Women in Business in Asia' in 2000 and subsequently ranked in the top 50 Women in Business internationally; by *Fortune* magazine in their first such listing in 2001 and subsequently in 2002, 2003 and 2006.

But today when Naina looks back, the satisfaction lies in the fact that successful women from her generation will be the role models for the coming generations.

India is emerging. The dogmas are disappearing at least in urban India and the aspiration to do better is arising in the women of rural India. Women who had to beg and plead their husbands to join SEWA to do some odd stitching jobs are today being cycled to other villages for work by their husbands. Some of them have even become *panchayti* leaders of their respective villages.

Limits and glass ceilings exist only in the mind now. However, women will at times, choose between family and work. It is not a glass ceiling, it is a personal choice.

"For Rishid's sake, who is very nervous about the day I retire, I will always keep doing something for a long time to come. He fears, I am going to drive him around the bench once I retire. Even when we are holidaying, while they are all struggling to get out of bed, I am up and ready and raring to go. I am always told, I am like a monkey on a hot brick roof-top. On a serious note, I may change track. I could be doing what my husband does."

After she has had her fill of corporate life, Naina is most inclined to join what has almost become the 'Kidwai tradition' of making life better for the women folk, through education and by creating means of employment, especially in rural India. She has witnessed through Rishid, how one can touch peoples' lives by very small contributions of time and resources. And maybe that is what Naina will do to complete the circle of life....plough back into the society, the well-being and prosperity that she has earned from it!

* * * * *

FOUR

Aspirations are Genetic

Neelam Dhawan

Managing Director, Microsoft India

A day before her board results were to be announced, Neelam Dhawan lay curled up in bed, feeling sick and miserable. She was making repeated but futile attempts to recall what she had written in the examination. But words had started swimming in her head and she was preparing herself for the worst. Finally, on the D-day, flanked by her parents and elder brother, she walked up to the school notice board to check her grades. She liked what she saw and thought she had done a decent job. As she was walking towards the car, she bumped into her mathematics teacher who hugged her and said she was proud of Neelam who had topped the school that year. Having survived the cramps and nightmares, Neelam silently allowed the victory to sink in. She slept a very satisfied soul that night.

Those were the days when internet was only what communication geeks could dream of and its mere existence was limited to the knowledge of bits and bytes in science fiction. Newspapers were the only one-stop-shop for information. So next morning, Neelam jumped out of bed, grabbed the day's newspaper and checked for her overall rank vis-à-vis other schools. The newspaper sprang a sweet surprise. Neelam was among the top rank holders across schools. She broke into a spring dance and banged at her parent's bedroom door to share her first major achievement in life. She felt fulfilled. For a child who took her studies more seriously than anything else in life, her only pursuit had been to have a sparkling score-card.

That day Neelam saw her name in the newspaper for the first time. But later in life, there were many more firsts to be added to her name, as she moved on to fight the tide to join the ranks of the first few successful career women in the country.

"As a child, I have that moment pinned up in my memory as my first few minutes of fame. It still feels the same every time I look at the newspaper that is one of the precious childhood souvenirs that I have saved."

Right Place, Wrong Era

Neelam was fortunate for she was a child born in a wrong era but in the right family. She was born on 22 October 1960 to Darshan Kumar and Kailash. Her father was in the services and had a hectic lifestyle. He used to keep phenomenal duty hours and it was quiet a challenge for the family not to have him around most of the time.

"Even though, we would hardly see him because of the job that he kept, he was fairly engaged in what we were doing. He was equally ambitious for my brother and me."

This was in the early 60s when India was yet to wake up to the potential of its women-power. But for Neelam, there were influences at home that provided a fertile ground for the seeds of ambition to germinate.

"My father's thought process was influenced by his sister who believed that women should be educated. Interestingly, even in that age and time, it was her firm belief that women must have a career of their own. That is what shaped my father's philosophy and induced him to think equally big for both the kids in the family. He wanted both of us to have a clear focus in life and never encouraged us to pursue useless pursuits even as children."

Neelam's father was a very self-conscious individual. He had a clear philosophy that guided him in bringing up his kids. "He would tell us: 'Nobody should say that I do not treat my daughter and son as equals. I cannot give lesser opportunity to my daughter as compared to my son.' So if my brother was pursuing higher education, I was also free to do that."

That was a difficult call to take in a social milieu where people were very conservative and daughters were not encouraged to pursue higher education. However, like most parents caught in the stereotype definitions of success, Neelam's parents wanted her to become a doctor. It came as a great disappointment to them when Neelam informed them of her lack of interest in the science subjects. She decided against taking science in high school.

"In school, I was the only kid who got the junior science talent award and that had probably given my parents the confidence that I was cut out for science and maybe medicine. But when I got up one day and told them that I don't have it in me to pursue science, they were truly dejected. They were angry in the beginning but finally respected my choice."

To Neelam, her mother Kailash was an even bigger influence than her dad. She had managed to finish her graduation despite coming from a family where she was one of four sisters and a brother.

"She loved literature and used to read a lot from Somerset Maugham to all the old classics. She would track people who would get the Nobel Prize and then try and read about their work. She loved music and I remember her as a very talented and accomplished woman. Later on, she wrote a few books for children in Hindi and she was very active till the time she died eighteen years ago."

As a guiding light, Neelam had her mother—a woman who graduated in the 50s, did self-study for the rest of her life and also authored books published for children, but to her regret, never got a chance to work in life.

"She believed that financial independence is very important for women. To her, if a woman is economically independent, emotional, cultural and social independence follows. She would always say if a woman has a career of her own, she is better equipped to face the vagaries of life. So till the time she died, she always looked upon my aunt who was a teacher and went on to become the headmistress of a school, with great regard."

Neelam's mother wished to see the potential that could not flower in her, blossom in her daughter. During her lifetime, Kailash could not push hard enough to make a career, but she kept telling Neelam not to repeat the mistake committed by her. With the stimulus at home, there was no way Neelam could sit back and watch the competitive world pass by. To compete was probably in her genes.

Parents always have the option to use their children as vessels into which they can pour either their failures or their aspirations. The philosophy of the parents goes a long way in shaping the future of their children as individuals. For Neelam, her father's sense of gender equality and mother's intellectual inclination, became a breeding ground of aspirations to do something worthwhile in life.

"I was a very aggressive individual, though I don't remember myself that way in early childhood. But as I touched the sixth grade, I became fiercely competitive. Life had already become a race. When I look back, I see myself as a child who was almost obsessed with being at the top of the class. Nothing else mattered in life. I would study hard imagining that there was someone else who was studying harder."

Neelam's benchmark was therefore, of her own making. She was focused, mission-driven and self-propelled. She would choose her object of desire—be it a toy or a book or a short-term objective—and then meticulously work towards achieving it. Over and above studies, hobbies were limited. Neelam would spend time either enacting plays on the terrace on summer afternoons with her gang of cousins or spending the entire afternoon playing monopoly. But for a larger part of her time, she would read what her mother would recommend—*War and Peace, Gone with the Wind, Pride and Prejudice,* and the likes.

"Unlike average parents, my mother initiated us into literature—which was very thought-provoking—quite early in life. We got exposed to paperback fiction much later in life. By then our thoughts had shaped up and we had matured."

But today a mother of two daughters, Neelam sees the different world through their eyes. "The present generation is much more wide-spread in their pursuits and ambitions. My younger daughter Nupur keeps asking 'What difference does it make whether I am at the top of the class or not'. And there was I, as a child loosing sleep, worrying about the person who would be working harder than I was and would beat me to the top. My parents never ever had to say a word to encourage me to study. I was self-propelled."

Stage Set for Action

As Neelam progressed in studies, she also recognized her yearning to be on the stage. Unfortunately, she never got selected to play any part as she was bad at theatrics.

But that did not douse her spirit. She could not act but spent equal amount of time and energy doing the preparations, getting the stage ready and handling the back-stage operations with finesse.

Neelam was quick to learn that if she failed to hone up her communication skills and expression, she would always have to stay back-stage in life. The realization dawned on her at St Stephen's College where she was studying economics and arts. She chanced upon an article on the importance of good communication skills to get somewhere in life and the failure encountered due to lack of expression. That was the turning point. Neelam knew she had to learn to conquer the stage and pushed herself into public speaking. She took to debating like there was no tomorrow.

"I was assisted by my teacher. She would instruct me to pick up a paragraph and just read it aloud to begin with. Initially, I struggled with it a lot but with practice, I pushed through and started participating in debates and elocutions. That exercise helped me clear my thought process and become a quick thinker. I gradually realized that these competitions are akin to life. You don't know what the next topic will be...whether you would be caught up in one situation or another...so you have to learn to be quick with the decision-making. And finally, it honed my communication skills and I started concentrating on every pause, focusing on diction, body language, expression, etc. I was enjoying myself thoroughly through the most rigorous communication training of my life."

Neelam's early years in college were disciplined and regimented with St Stephens being one college which was paranoid about academics. There was the normal rig amour—attendance, December examinations, and tutorials. It was more like an extension of school and there was no time to loiter around.

"I do not remember a day when I would have bunked school to do something else. One thing that hits you there is the fact that everyone around is a topper from his or her school. That is like a self-propeller and you get into that competitive environment without having to try very hard."

The other big change she remembers from that phase in her life is the fact that Neelam went to a girls' school. But now she was in a co-education environment and it was time to test whether she was comfortable with boys around.

"On hindsight, I think it is a bad idea to put women in an all-girls school. It took me quite some time to make friends and break the ice with the opposite sex; even though they were very well-meaning individuals from very competitive backgrounds, I had grown up with a mental block that took a lot of time to overcome. I started loosening up a bit in the second year but it took quite an effort to shake a mindset off."

Grief is Hard to Handle

Around that time, came Neelam's most important lesson in life but this one was from outside college. But, this exposure was to go a long way in shaping her up as a compassionate and responsible citizen. Mother Teresa was visiting Delhi. Neelam, for the first time, registered the kind of work she did. She was also influenced by one of her seniors in college studying English (Hons), who was actively involved in missionary activities. Neelam saw a new direction and decided to take a peep into the lives of the deprived around her.

The Missionaries of Charity had set up an orphanage and an old age home in Delhi. Neelam and her friend used to go to the old age home after college to spend some time with the elderly who had nowhere to go in the dusk of their lives.

"For the first time in life, I learned that it is not easy to handle grief. The old people's home was depressing and it needed a lot of moral and emotional courage to console the people who had nothing to look forward to in life. I could not handle it and maybe, did not have the emotional maturity to live through the experiences without feeling completely devastated myself. My parents got worried and upset as I would cry a lot after every visit. They too thought that I needed some more emotional stability before I could share somebody else's grief."

So Neelam decided to move to 'preventive intervention' in the society by giving time to children who were struggling to make a life at the orphanage. The kids used to go to St Xavier's and Presentation Convent and it was a little difficult for them to handle studies without help. So Neelam started teaching them mathematics.

"It gave me a strange sense of fulfillment and a confidence that I could contribute in someone's life. I realized how, as an individual, I could make a small difference to the lives of people around me. That also gave me emotional maturity and stability. Somehow, the sense of giving drives internal peace as there is a realization that there are people who can gain from you and there are people who are worst off. That realization is very important to keep you rooted. After that experience, I could never take what came to me for granted. I have learned to appreciate each and every little thing that comes my way as God's grace."

The Worldwide Ocean

By the time Neelam had started pursuing her management studies at the Faculty of Management Studies Delhi University, she was a more mature individual with the realization that life is not all about score-cards. You win some, you lose some and it is more important to play the game and enjoy every bit of it.

"I was more comfortable with life and its many shades by then. The rat race had become less important. So, at times I would join the gang to bunk college and go for a movie or to watch a play. I think I felt more balanced as an individual."

Being a good student and despite the distractions, she still did well in management and specialized in Marketing and Operational Research. She did not top the class but was leading in her specializations.

Finally, it was placement season and companies started visiting the campus for recruitment. But it was a season of shock for Neelam. At a point where even the candidates from the lowest rung of merit had got their offer letters, Neelam was still struggling to get a foothold. She was absolutely confused. Gradually, she figured out that the reason for the lack of interest on the part of the recruiters was her specialization in marketing.

It was 1992, but to Neelam's surprise, corporate India was still not comfortable with having women in sales and marketing. Even India's largest companies, who came on campus, showed regret as they did not take women in those functional areas. Neelam was devastated. She had two options to choose from—one was with a bank where the money would be good but it was not a sales and marketing job. The other was with an upcoming

Soulmate: Atul Dhawan has proved to be an ideal partner

information technology bellwether called HCL for a sales and marketing job.

"I decided to go with the company who was ready to place their bets on a woman in sales and marketing. Also my brother encouraged me to participate in the information technology sector that was nascent and developing at a very fast pace. He felt, I could contribute more in this sector than in banking where women had already made a mark."

Back then, HCL Technologies was not as evolved as they are today. Those were the early days when IBM had left India and there was HCL, DCM and Wipro on the information technology horizon and they were all grappling with a new area of business.

"There were two ladies in the company—one in systems and the other one was me. The regional manager, whom I was to report to, struggled for quite some time trying to figure out what role he should be assigning me. But these were the early days of women trying to make a career and his plight was understandable. In any case, women had not quite started going on sales and marketing calls and he was totally at a loss of precedent.

First two years were tough for the management and they were finding it more difficult to handle my profile than I was finding it to manage marketing calls. I was not perturbed. Time is a good tester. A few months down the line, they too started getting comfortable with having me around. After the signing of the first few deals, I became more acceptable. And then things could only get better.

The industry was small and growing each passing day and there were lots of young and bright people joining it, fortunately many of them being women."

In Neelam's case, the struggle within HCL was not so much about her being a woman as HCL even then was a company of equal opportunity, but it was more to do with her not being an engineer. People were comfortable with women being engineers but this one was aspiring something that had still not become the norm. Neelam was wanting to excel in marketing, negotiating service -level agreements, closing contracts for the company, and bringing in business.

There were softer cultural issues that would crop up and make things very amusing for the lady. "The 'all men' brotherhood was struggling to adjust to my presence after I joined. I remember walking into a regional manager's room one evening. He had his feet up on his table. He made a face and very grudgingly put his feet down."

But in her new calling, Neelam's rigorous training in communication from school came very handy. She found it very easy to connect to peers and customers who were very supportive. "After I got HCL the first deal and got into the selling and supporting cycle, customers started feeling comfortable with having me around. The fact that you could actually influence the buying decisions in very large companies, gave me the confidence to put my foot on the accelerator."

Now that Neelam looks back, she appreciates that for every successful woman trying the ropes of business in that era, there had to be people or companies who would bet on their merit and show confidence in them. The women who entered into the fray at that time were brave but the companies who gave them their trust were braver.

A couple of years after Neelam joined HCL, the company was working on the project to launch a personal computer in India for the first time. No one had ever sold a PC in India till then.

"I was too young in the company, but I think they risked it with me by giving me the responsibility to roll out this product that was very crucial for the company. Working on the project brought me very close to the top management as I was under a very close watch. The company was investing crores into the project. So they were keeping a close eye on how I was handling the launch."

Neelam knew she had to make it happen. The team would work till 3 in the morning with reams of paper and documents, having no e-mails and messengers to help them communicate remotely. She dabbled with billboards and roadshows for the first time and travelled across the country to anchor the launch. The success of the project made way for Neelam to stay with the company for 13 years.

"But I clearly understand my limitations and why I got very lucky in my pursuit. I could not have done what Vinita Bali does as I would not probably be able to break ice with people in other sectors like FMCG or consumer durables. I got lucky with this sector. In IT, even your channel partners and vendors are very well educated. The awareness levels are so high that a sales call can become a pleasure. It was a new sector and we were all learning together. Also in the 80s, the decision-makers in IT implementations were people usually at the level of CEO or financial directors. That was always a different class of people from whom one would learn each passing day."

In 1995, Neelam moved on to IBM that had re-entered India and had been here for a couple of years in partnership with the Tatas. She joined them for the server business but went on to head the PC business for the company.

"IBM is a company where the 'old boys' culture is very well entrenched. The longer you stay, the better you learn and I did learn a lot."

After heading the server business and later the PC business at IBM, Neelam got the offer to head the complete Sales and Marketing for the PC division of Compaq. It was a good opportunity as the usage of PCs in India was gaining momentum and Compaq was in the heat of activity.

Professional Pangs

Neelam was heading the sales for Compaq India when Hewlett-Packard announced its intent to acquire Compaq. To pull through that merger unscathed became Neelam's worst nightmare. While in the US, the merger witnessed rough weather due to the promoters not agreeing to it. Back home, it unsettled the apple cart for Compaq and its employees and customers alike.

"The period between the intention of the merger being announced till the time it closed (it was announced in September 2004 and closed in May 2005) was a real testing time for the Compaq team. Mergers always bring some amount of uncertainty and uncertainties are very demotivating. On one hand, the news unsettled the employees who would come and ask me if they had a future with the company and on the other hand, consumers had to be assured there would be no break in service.

My team would come and ask me if they would be able to keep their jobs and customers had to be reassured that things were not going to change for them. That was a tough call in a scenario where I myself was not sure where the company was headed. The fact is you can't play with people's careers or even the faith that customers have put in you."

But both Compaq and Neelam weathered the storm. The Indian part of the business did well despite the unfavourable circumstances.

"Compaq was up for acquisition but business did not slack. We did not lose customers and that could probably be one of the reasons why the Indian Compaq team got senior management positions with Hewlett-Packard. Those were very difficult times but we didn't lose momentum or people and we sailed through."

Where do you Want to go Today

By now Neelam had proven her credentials enough to catch the attention of the Big Daddy in the IT world—Microsoft. All along Neelam was a hardware person, but now she also was ready to move to a company that had a macro vision to do something different. She wanted to move to a role where she could have a large impact rather than just influencing a few sales decisions. Microsoft offered her the bait. She was offered the position of managing director where she had to oversee the complete business. And she warmed up to the position without much trepidation.

"I do not think running Microsoft is more taxing than running any sales operation as in either case you have different set of targets to meet, though they are on a much larger scale and multi-dimensional in case of a company like Microsoft.

At Microsoft, it's important to understand what perceptions people carry of us as a technology or a company and I truly believe that makes a large chunk of what I do. In sales, you influence buying decisions directly; in heading a company, you influence perceptions about the company and its products that indirectly influence buying decisions. In a way, you become the ambassador for the company and sometimes even the product category, especially when you are carrying the banner of a company as big as Microsoft."

The Mommy Material

Throughout this journey, the only constant in this professional woman's life is the balancing act between home and work. Whatever be the role, the tight rope has to be scaled by every woman. And for women, the priority list changes on a day to day basis.

"If your kid is sick, that is your priority for the day…if you need to travel to sign a deal, that is the priority for the day…..so a woman's life is very dynamic. On certain days, the exams of the kids are more important and on others, a series of presentations takes precedence. And it is God's grace that women are very good at multi-tasking. They have the flair to manage difficult and diverse situations."

And Neelam learned to do the balancing act right from the time she met the Mr Right of her life. "I met

In her two daughters, Naina and Nupur, Neelam gets to taste all facets of the present generation

my husband through my aunt. We have some common friends but it was actually the aunts who brought us together. His aunt and my aunt went to college together. They thought we could pair up well so we started seeing each other."

Six months down the line, the two were happily married and since then, Atul Dhawan—who by profession is a partner with Delloitt—has lived up to her expectation of being the ideal soulmate.

"When we finally decided to take back the news home about our decision to marry, I asked him if he had any problems with my working. But that was a silly question and he sounded surprised."

Acceptance of women working in the family came very naturally to him. His mother was a career woman and had set up a business in 1958 and when Neelam got married, she was still working. So the question was uncalled for. And since then, he remains one person who shares both her professional and personal ups and downs.

The couple is blessed with two daughters, the elder one Naina is 18 and the younger, Nupur, is 15. But as is true with every mother of her generation, Neelam finds it difficult to cope with a generation that studies with the music turned on, chats open and messengers on.

"This generation was not born for scoring grades and maintaining credits. Their world is like the world wide web. It has everything and there are no boundaries. I see that even the three-year difference between my two daughters brings in a vast change in the way they think.

Unlike our generation, kids these days start worrying about what they want to do in life much later in life and they seem to be much more distracted."

But in her two daughters, Neelam gets to taste all facets of the present generation with the younger one being an extrovert who loves western music and is always excited about getting dressed and the elder daughter who is extremely focused, tuned into Bollywood and who likes her close coterie of friends.

"Initially, I tried to impose upon them the regime that I had followed as a teenager. But Atul advised me not to push them. He believes that every individual finds his own levels and I realize that he was right. Both the kids are now growing into wonderful and responsible individuals and thankfully are not growing under the shadows of successful professionals as parents."

Unique Success Proposition

"I do not think I am a very strategic person and I could never think straight as a strategist. I would call myself more of an executor of strategies. If the company is clear in its head on where it needs to be, I can get on the top of the situation and do whatever it takes to get it there."

This is the quality that has helped Neelam create a niche for herself in the Indian IT landscape. And undoubtedly, her years in sales and marketing have made her an immaculate and brilliant networker. She connects instantly and intelligently.

"The other most important strength is that I have a very tolerant nature. The situation has to be really bad for me to yell at someone or something. So, I am very cool by nature. If someone has made an error, I know there is always a way of working around it and it does not tick me off. I talk to the person, discuss it, but never hold it against him or her. That has also helped me make friends in my professional life. I could never have done it if I would have gone around with a chip on my shoulder.

Sometimes, I feel I am a little more forgiving than I should be but that helps me keep my cool, especially as a woman boss. It was a long time ago that I got sensitized to the need to be more understanding about the mind-set of the people working with me. At any given point in time, there are people reporting to me, who are much more senior in the profession. All of them would have wanted my job. My direct team wants my job too! I have learned to appreciate that. So I think the best way is to guide them on how to get there and the other more important and critical part is to respect somebody's seniority and give the person the credit for his knowledge and experience. It is bound to breed mutual respect."

And along the way, she faced challenges that were more cultural than professional. "One of my senior colleagues at IBM had something weighing on him so we decided to sit and chat. What he told me was a shocker for me. He said, he couldn't go back home and tell his family that his boss was a woman. They would just not accept it. But that was the reality of the situation, he was a senior and his boss was a woman, junior in age and experience and he was feeling embarrassed to mention this fact at home."

However, there is also the other side of the coin. Being a woman sometimes also added more compassion into the culture where she was working. "The other day, a colleague's wife called up and said she had called only to thank me. She felt that having a woman boss had changed a lot in her husband's thinking and life. 'Earlier, his boss would call at 10 pm and he would be on the phone till 11 in the night irrespective of where he was or what we were doing as a family. There would be meetings on Saturdays and Sundays without any respect for the family's private time. But all that has changed', she said."

For Neelam, her working on a Saturday does not mean everyone has to work. As a woman, it is easier to identify with the needs of an average family to be together and bond whenever there is time. "When people are leaving work after 8 in the evening, there is no point in calling them again at 10 when they are just getting home. If the skies are not falling and the thing can wait till the next day, I do not call them."

Dress to Conquer

Neelam loves to celebrate life and that is why everyday before she steps out of her home, she takes one good look at the mirror to make sure everything is in order. She dresses with the day's engagements in mind. If its a day of meetings with government representatives or partners, then it will be a sari—nicely pleated and elegantly carried to add seriousness to her profile. If it is a media event, there is need to dress with visual appeal in mind.

"For me, dressing has a lot to do with my confidence levels. When I step out of the house, I have to be absolutely confident about the way I am dressed and the way I look. There is no place for shabby dressing in my life. I love beads and have an amazing collection of the same. If there is a bead that I can afford to buy, I would have bought it by now. I spend a lot of money on the paraphernalia and I love to match my dress with the required accessories. I am an absolute woman at heart and I cannot carry any pretence about that."

And that is where she loves to spend money occasionally—shopping for herself and the girls, though she confesses that the girls hardly ever like what she buys. But that does not stop her. Recently, while going shopping for jewellery, she asked Atul to accompany her. "He was very amused and kept asking me why I wanted him to be there. He felt the piece may be so exorbitant that I wanted him to foot the bill."

Sweet Compromises

For any career woman, it is impossible to duck the stress of keeping a family and a job balanced. There is always a give and take. "My family has always been very supportive. My second daughter was three months old when my mother-in-law stopped working. She said she wanted to be with them and that was a great help and probably that is what kept me going. In the absence of any organized child care in India at that time, I could not have brought up my girls in the hands of untrained help. And I certainly could not have done without the supervision of my in-laws.

As far as staying away from the family and maintaining a hectic schedule is concerned, my children are quite used to my travelling or being away as they have grown up seeing me like this. Initially, I used to worry when I was travelling. But then, my mother-in-law told me: 'They cry when they see you but five minutes after you leave, they forget you completely. It is out of sight, out of mind for kids.' That gave me some consolation and I started feeling less miserable about leaving them and going.

Now they are so used to me working that if I stay home for more than two days, I start getting into their hair. They get upset when I ask them to do this and that. They actually keep asking me: 'Why are you not going to work? Don't you have e-mails to clear?' They want me out of their way."

Neelam agrees that there have been minor compromises but nothing that she could not live around. "In life there are a few things that do get left behind when one is trying to run but I had prioritized job, family and social responsibilities. Somewhere my home did get neglected a bit. I press the panic buttons on something at the home front only if things are breaking down and need immediate attention. But that is fine and I do not carry any guilt on that one. I am more focused on the people in my family than the things around me."

And as far as connecting with people is concerned, times have changed drastically. Physical distances do not mean anything anymore. "Naina is in the US and we use internet and videoconferencing to speak to her and see her. Whenever I am clearing my mails on my way back from work, she suddenly pops up on the messenger and we end up chatting about the special and the routine that has happened in our lives during the day. There is no communication gap. Modern tools are so effective. Now they have me on the 'Facebook' and we participate in each other's lives even when we are not together physically."

But Neelam is an honest mother. "I think the communication has been good from my side and we always connected with each other and they did not mind my career pursuit. But frankly, I have never gathered enough courage to ask them if they missed me because if they were to say yes, then what was I to do? I did not play this game to give up. If that question means giving up my career, I would rather skirt it."

But the most important fact is that when she is with them on family vacations or on weekends cooking a family meal, she is completely devoted to them.

Picture perfect: Neelam is more focussed on the people in her family than materialistic pursuits

To Neelam, her biggest blessing is her happy-go-lucky nature that never allows her to get stressed. "It takes a lot to get me stressed. The only unpleasant experience is if the kids are not putting in enough work or if one of us is unwell. Otherwise, I am never on the edge. And with age, I have also learned to switch to a much healthier lifestyle. I go to the gym and have become very conscious of what I eat. That has added to the feel-good factor and helps me keep stress at bay."

All these years in IT has given Neelam's personality a very matter-of-fact, no nonsense flavour—a plug-and-play attitude where the rules are straight and simple. The 'follow the Sun' work schedule may be testing but she takes each challenge that comes her way like a bug in an algorithmic solution. Her short-term dream is to make the benefits of IT available to the last person on the street at an affordable price. And that is what she sees herself working on in the times to come.

* * * * *

FIVE

The Indian Weaver-bird

Ritu Kumar

Fashion Designer

Ritu Kumar is a modern-day designer whose label is patronized not just by India's bold and the beautiful but also by international style icons like Jemima Khan and late Princess Diana. But a larger part of Ritu still lives in an era of the ruling dynasties of India, sharing the spirit of the spinners, weavers, dyers, printers and embroiderers. She has spent a better part of her career studying craft forms of the bygone era.

Much of the patronage extended to the skilled craftsmen in that era came from the royalty. So her study got extended into the realms of the royal lifestyle where the costumes of the kings, queens and the courtiers mirrored the social fabric—delicate muslin from Dhaka, fine silk brocades from Varanasi, complex woollen weaves from Kashmir, intricate gold embroideries from Lahore.

Most would know Ritu Kumar as a designer who created a home-grown fashion brand for India. Very few, however, would know the other side of her personality —the historian in her who has spent years tracing the evolution of the Indian costume and the fabric that goes into its making. She, for instance, discovered during her research that cotton fabric along with its embellished forms was the first product category to be exported out of pre-independence India, in addition to spices that the country was famous for.

During her journey through the various fabrics woven in time, she learned about the people of India and their relationship with the environment. Thanks to her passion, she has revisited the splendid traditional textiles which gave the country a self-sustained enterprise and offered livelihood to generations, right from 2500 BC till India finally lost it to the commercial interests of the British Empire.

"There is a lot we lost after the death of royal rituals during and after the British rule and with it died the ceremonial costumes and the tradition that fed the Indian economy from the very beginning. It was not just the territories of the Maharajas that merged into a single democratic state. The individual creative skills that had been handed down generations of craftsmen also merged into the oblivion. To me, the loss of that skill-set is one of the biggest historical losses for post-independence India."

Unfortunately, with the disappearance of royal rituals, the traditional and ceremonial costumes were packed away in trunks, donated to museums, sold to private collectors or just left to decay. But if Ritu had her way, she would see all of them mingle into the contemporary designs that she creates today. She stands as an ambassador of the age-old skills of growing, spinning, weaving, dying and 'patterning' of cotton. She patronizes the ancient art of unstitched silk and is spearheading the resurrection of stitching, styling, ornamenting and detailing of fabric.

Over the years, her contemporary take on traditional crafts, has become her signature and she has succeeded in giving Indian traditional crafts, an aspirational value of a brand. Though in a small way, she started the trend that has breathed life into a small portion of the dying cult of an estimated 1,60,00,000 crafts people living in many sleepy hamlets all across India. The magic in their fingers has once again started to create a well-deserved fan-following.

She also has the distinction of being the first woman, who some thirty-five years ago, introduced the 'boutique' culture in India under the brand name 'Ritu's Boutique'. Today, she has outlets in all major cities in India. But beyond the commercial success as a first-generation entrepreneur, her profile is rather heavy. She is an anthropologist and a museologist rolled into one. She has been in the hinterlands with a sensitive spade, digging into the history of Indian costume, unearthing the secrets of the rich handicraft tradition lost in time, brushing cobwebs from the commercial heritage that India lost to British colonization. She is showcasing it in her work but in parallel, she is also documenting the journey of the Indian threads of creativity.

"I am celebrating the global success of Indian fashion, styling and design because the industry is unsuspectingly taking with it the craftsmen who had been isolated for centuries. Indian *Shilpashastra* is getting another chance."

For Ritu, it has so far been a long journey of discovery both of self as well as India's textile heritage that was. But her destination clearly is the rediscovery and documentation of the craft-forms that have been running in the Indian fingers for centuries.

Beginning Blues

Ritu's family lived in Amritsar in Punjab and for sometime in Kashmir, but mostly in areas where there were no good schools and in an era when schools were not necessarily meant for girls. But her family was liberal and culturally enlightened.

"We lived in a very large joint family so it was a very comfortable life with lots of cousins to play with and number of aunts and uncles to look after us. Unfortunately, there were no good schools in the area where we lived. So I had to be sent to a boarding very early on—almost from kindergarten onwards."

Born on 11 November 1944, Ritu's childhood is a combination of warm memories of phases split between her hearth and Tara Hall in Shimla. "We had a fairly close family but extremely liberated in terms of their thinking. My uncles were part of the freedom struggle. So there was a lot of emphasis on education. School was magic and fond memories of the beautiful mountain peaks keep coming back to me even now."

Ritu's parents, Puran and Leela Mehta, originally from Pakistan were very loving, warm and extremely understanding about her desire to do different things at different stages in life. "They understood why I needed to be brought back from a boarding school, where I was sent in kindergarten, due to homesickness. And later they respected my wish to move out of Amritsar to wider pastures in Delhi and then to America for further studies. There was no gender bias in the family and girls were treated as equals."

As a student, Ritu does not remember herself as a very studious child. "I have always enjoyed my work—in school and college. I wasn't very studious in the conventional sense of the term and was naughty and something of a mad-cap as well. But, one good thing is that I normally took to whatever I did. I could get really involved in something I liked."

Ritu had all along wanted to study arts, especially history. But her parents thought that there was more seriousness and discipline in the science faculty at Panjab University and after years in boarding school, they were in no mood to send their daughter out to another destination. Since it was early days of higher education for women, the important calls were still taken by the family. So, she studied science and math, and scored the highest marks in the university even though the two subjects were hardly her favourites. But Ritu, has all along been more focused on the end and not on the means to an end. She would do whatever hard work it took to excel in what she thought was important to accomplish.

"I believe if you have the basic intelligence and are ready to take up a task diligently, you can do just about anything. It might not be as enjoyable as your favourite pursuits but it's equally enriching and 'doable'."

From Panjab University, Ritu moved out to Delhi. Here again the influence of her family came into play in choosing Lady Irwing over Miranda House.

"I was sent to Lady Irwing which offered a very dull course in Home Science. On hindsight, it was the best thing that could have happened to me as the college offered an exchange scholarship programme and I won the scholarship to go to Briarcliff Manor in New York Westchester County. In a way, this is the phase where my actual education started in my desired areas of pursuit. I studied the history of art and drama and that actually steered the course of my future."

Ritu returned to India with the realization of how little she knew of her own country and heritage. She had been quizzed about India while in America and that had pushed her to make an extra effort to know and understand her country better. "Initially I was embarrassed by how little I knew about my country. So, I was actually forced into studying about India and its rich past."

Brush with Kolkata

After her stint in America, Ritu returned to Delhi and married Shashi Kumar, whom she had met during her college days in Delhi. His sister Uma Kumar had studied with Ritu. They had known each other for years so the bonding had stood the test of time. Ritu moved to Kolkata after marrying Shashi.

After she got married, she found herself in a very sophisticated and literary atmosphere that encouraged her to join the University of Calcutta to pursue a course in Indian history and art. It was early times for women to dabble with any such abstract calling and the course itself was obscure. The course actually had to do with Museology—an understanding of the exhibits in a museum which includes studying a wide range of art forms like sculptures, paintings and different crafts. In fact, the only one of its type offered was by Ashutosh Museums because they had a museum in the college. There were only three students in the class.

During the course of this study, she pursued archeological projects and got an exposure to the mechanics of art and history and how data was processed from ancient sites. This actually, became the genesis of Ritu's interest in the various craft forms.

"I can't exactly put my finger on it but I know that my interest in crafts started subconsciously around the same time."

Shashi lost his father in the first year of their marriage. They had to start earning a living and support themselves. Shashi started working and Ritu started a small store in Kolkata. She began her production work with four hand-block printers and two tables in a small village near Kolkata.

Destiny Knocked

At her small Kolkata store, destiny did knock one day. Ritu got an order to deliver 2,000 pieces of a scarf that she was showcasing at the tiny store. She developed cold feet. The scale of the order was not something she could manage on her own. She needed support to organize the man-days in different villages for the craftsmen to deliver the order well in time and of a quality that would meet the expectation of her first international client. So far, it had been a few pieces at a time, a couple of thousand pieces seemed to be out of bounds. But the opportunity was God sent, so it could not be ignored.

Shashi, in any case, did not like his mundane job much, so he offered to help. The couple got together to execute their first international order. He brought coherence into the work flow and helped Ritu to get the act together. After that there was no looking back. It became a career for both.

That was the beginning of 'Ritu's Boutique'—a company under the proprietorship of Ritu Kumar. In 1977, it was converted into a partnership concern under the banner of Ritika Private Limited. The company finally adopted its trademark and logo Ritu Kumar in April 2001. Currently, Ritika Private Limited operates two main production centres in Gurgaon and Kolkata. The factories are equipped with in-house printing, tailoring, finishing and quality control facilities.

A few years from the humble beginning, Ritu became an established brand and she has lots of proud moments as a first-generation entrepreneur, tucked away safely into her portfolio. In 1998, she bagged the 'Outstanding Women Entrepreneur Award' by the PHD-Chamber of Commerce that was to be followed by 'Lifetime Achievement Award' by the Kingfisher Group, Achievement Award by National Institute of Fashion Technology, the 'Glam Womenswear (Indian) Designer' by Tuscan Verve Zoom Glam Awards. More recently, she bagged The Limca Yearly Award in 2007 and The Indira Gandhi Priyadarshani Award in 2008.

Seeing Red

Ritu scaled up the business but not without initial teething troubles. Kolkata being Kolkata, even her small factory there started having a troubled union. There was a strike and the Communist Party of India (Marxist) did a closure on it despite the fact that it was a cottage industry. "We could not figure out how we could face a closure like that. But we had no means to fight and eventually had to shut shop."

Fortunately, when Ritu had started work in Kolkata in the 70s, she had opened the first Ritu's Boutique in Delhi with the supplies coming from her tiny hand-block unit in the villages near Kolkata. Therefore, the couple had the option and relocated in Delhi. That suited them professionally as all export work was sourced out of Delhi in those days given the difficult work culture of Kolkata which only a few businesses could survive.

However, something kept taking Ritu back to the 'city of joy'. She kept revisiting the villages and realized there was little work there and the crafts-people she saw had lost patronage and identity. They were slipping economically. This prompted Ritu to collect enough courage and she commenced the Kolkata operations again. The store had always been there but Ritu had stopped production work in Kolkata. She restarted production and this time the people who had worked with her earlier started managing the operations and still continue to do so.

As Ritu interacted with a cross-section of craftsmen and artisans across Kolkata, and subsequently in many states across India, she realized that there was an undocumented repertoire of knowledge and skills that was waiting to be revisited. "There was no documented evidence of the designs that were native to a number of areas whether they were related to prints, weave, or embroidery. I had no way to trace back a single motif, if I wanted to."

This pursuit exposed Ritu to a very moving story of the death of some of the best Indian crafts. The 200 years of colonial rule had ensured that most fabric sold in India was a copy of indigenous design but produced in Lancashire in England and re-exported to India. The regions of their origin, where silk hand-worked scarves had started selling cheaper than mill-made polyester ones, were hopelessly impoverished. This had forced the crafts-families into despair and abject poverty.

Interestingly, as Ritu's association with the crafts-villages deepened, she found herself leading one life of glamour in urban India and another, a more sombre and rooted one in rural India—but the latter was not known even to her closest friends.

"I was earning my living. But that was gradually becoming peripheral to what I was discovering as a researcher. I started scouting for material in other parts of India. My initial research for prints began in the 60s. I took several trips to Rajasthan, UP, and Delhi. In Delhi, I met people who were working in an atmosphere charged with national pride. Spearheaded by Kamaladevi Chattopadhyaya and Pupul Jayakar, most of us including Laila Tyabji, Martand Singh, Rajesh Thakore, and Rajiv Sethi were searching for our roots with earnestness of purpose but in our own characteristic way. I, in particular, was looking for examples of classical fabrics."

Before she realized, Ritu had embarked upon a journey where there were no paths, no footprints to follow and no foghorns or lighthouses. There was little material for study and textile museums in India, at that time, were few and far between.

"Most old clothing with the royal homes dates to a confused sartorial 20th century baroque textiles period. But what I was looking for was a Renaissance. It was hard work but extremely satisfying and exciting. It sometimes took years to track a design back to its roots but when that happened, miraculous jewelled textiles emerged from long forgotten textile districts."

Ritu's first exhibition of saris using designs from India's renowned print schools was held in Kolkata. Of 30 researched pieces, she managed to sell only a dozen, over four days. She realized she had gone wrong. No one wanted to buy a print that looked like a Farukhabad bedcover on thick handloom cotton. That was apt for the women in the 18th century but for the new-look Indian women, it was unacceptable to dress like a tea cozy.

That was Ritu's first lesson as a designer. One could not plant the 18th century idioms straight into the 20th century. The lesson: 'Use the idiom, motif, the design and all that made that school of design so magnificent, but dovetail it to contemporary style and aspirations.'

Learning Along the Way

She was in her 20s and her other big lesson in life came from Pupul Jayakar who headed The Handloom and Handicraft Board then and was one of the pioneers of what can be called 'the revival movement'.

Ritu had discovered a huge lexicon of designs with a family of block makers who had trunks full of designs on crumbling paper, preserved perhaps from the 18th century. The family's traditional livelihood had vanished but the old grandfather had the genius.

"It was a levelling experience, as I watched him draw a diagonal pattern on a block 4" × 4" which transported me back to the art school. He had learned the skill of 'patterning' from his forefathers who, he claimed, carved and designed patterns which imprinted fabrics, which were exported in dhows to the Arab world and further abroad, in the 17th century."

In her excitement, Ritu rushed to Pupul Jayakar to share her discovery. Jayakar said: "There is a need to unearth and sustain this legacy in every district in this country. Unless your generation is willing to understand that this is your heritage and that it is slipping through your hands, there can be no awakening. Do not come running to me. Do something about it."

What fuelled the mission was Ritu's association with like-minded people who would occasionally ask her to pitch in for some projects that they were undertaking in some remote area. That would trigger off a new association and new success story for a handful of crafts-people in areas like Maheshwar, Lucknow, Machillipatnam, Benaras, Ahmedabad, Sanganer, Kanchipuram, Bhuj, Tharparkar—an amazing kaleidoscope of rich textile resources— and the journey kept taking her to design destinations unheard of and unexplored.

Ritu is relentlessly redefining the term 'fashion' in the Indian context

"The sequence of events is blurred in my mind, but I certainly know that the visits to the remote villages intrigued me. I just went with the flow and I got more and more interested when I did some revival work in some area and went back to check what impact it had on the lives of the craftsmen living there."

Ritu was visiting these villages to keep business going as well as unearthing traditional knowledge. But unknowingly, she got pushed into a frame where she started witnessing the economic impact that even a little amount of business made in these areas. Especially, the small orders that she was bringing to the villages was empowering women. This started giving Ritu a heady feeling.

"I got drawn into it more and more. I have to confess that it was out of no philanthropic reasons that I had started working in these areas, there was no blueprint and it wasn't social projects that I was working on. But, slowly over the years, when I saw the impact that it had made in their lives, I just couldn't snap the association." In 1988, one of Ritu's craftsmen earned the President's Award for excellence in the craft of hand-block printing.

Picking Up the Textile Threads

The collective bait in the villages was deadly. She travelled across India for reasons that were commercial and also for her research and last but not the least, to get a sense of fulfillment by empowering craft communities in the remotest nook and corner across India.

As she discovered bits and pieces of the Indian textile heritage, scattered in the remotest parts across India, she kept getting more frustrated about how we had allowed this priceless possession to get fragmented due to national neglect. There was no documentation and the story seemed to be lost forever.

"I started going to the museums abroad and I think that is where the seed of a book was sown. I remember realizing that in one's career, one would move on without leaving any information for anyone else to tread the same path. Anyone who would start would have to re-invent the wheel as there was no documentation or a historical trail to follow."

The realization led to the book *Costumes and Textiles of Royal India* published by Christies in October 1999 that chronicles the history of textiles and art design in India—a book that is a definite and exhaustive academic reference point for the fashion history.

Winds of Change

When Ritu started, there was nothing called fashion. The likes of Ritu Kumar and Rajiv Sethi were barefoot doctors pursuing craftwork—all of them working in different disciplines. Kamaladevi Chattopadyay and Pupul Jayakar would tell them to go to some remote place where they could find a printing village, a legacy of a performing artist, a potter's village and each, with their own interest, would start working in the village, incorporating the craft forms into their work and their calling. There was no glamour, no magnified mention of the work that they did in contemporary media. It was a simple means of livelihood and interest—just another calling.

"When I was asked to participate in an exhibition mounted at the Lalit Kala Academy by Ms Swantantra Prakash, I was in awe of the invitation. I did not believe someone would be interested in a theme like researched contemporary versions of patterned fabrics of India.

Those were the days when if you did get a mention in any of the media articles that were published about an exhibition, it was focused on the art form and not the artist. There was no or perhaps a tiny mention of the designer in the footnote, but much more for what we were—a catalyst and not the creator. Those days there was no Page 3 audience nor was the electronic media all pervasive."

Things have changed. In the past decade, it's the media and very attractive images on the ramp that has created a very different image of fashion. But the media glare and the merging of fashion borders has also lead to an identity crisis in the sector, with cross pollination of regional and Western styles, resulting in fresh new design vocabularies that are not always relevant in the Indian context.

With the result, today Ritu stands as a lady holding a small glimmering light to the rich Indian cultural identity woven into the classicism of textiles. But she is faced by the glaring lights of media and western fashion and hundreds of MNC brands that have gradually invaded the psyche of the rich and the fashionable in India, making it a tough call.

She is relentlessly redefining the term 'fashion' in the Indian context. Most importantly, she has demonstrated that the products of the work of the hand can be as profitable as and even more glamorous than the machine-made ones. Indian fashion is more than capable of holding it's own in the international arena of haute couture.

But all this has to be put in perspective. Therefore, documenting this legacy of textile and costumes of an older order chronologically is the most logical step for Ritu. She is working backwards to get to the era of handcrafted creativity. Ritu has collected priceless collection of textile and design both from 20th century and earlier and is looking forward to mounting them in a museum for reference by others who are interested in the Indian heritage.

"There are also four or five volumes that are begging to be written about this country's textile heritage. And I will also put my mind to a book that will put the 40-50 years of Indian fashion into perspective."

Through her designs, she is celebrating the spirit of the bygone era and its splendour woven into an array of threads. She is reinventing the world's richest repertoire of hand-crafted textiles for use in modern India—a brand that is already setting global ramps on fire with its creative prowess. Ritu wants to take full advantage of this exposure.

"The visibility has become very high and very often out of proportion to what the event is. But I am not complaining because the fashion industry has, by default, become a very strong marketing tool for the Indian crafts without intending to do so. No one person could have promoted the efforts of these craftsmen but the growing industry and its rip off has promoted their work too."

Chak de India

In the past half a decade, Ritu has seen 'Brand India' come a long way. Earlier, when Ritu used to travel abroad, nobody was even ready to accept her visiting card. 'Made in India' was a no no! India was one poor banana republic of a country and was more an embarrassment as a business destination and a sourcing base. But today India's time has come. The richer nations have started looking up to Indians and treating their talent with respect.

Since 1994, Ritu has been designing wardrobes comprising swimwear, evening wear, traditional Indian wear, casual wear, formal evening gowns of the three winning Miss Indias for their participation in International Beauty Pageants like Miss Universe, Miss World and Miss Asia Pacific. Some of the winners in these events have won awards for the Most Outstanding Evening Gown and the Best National Costume. This has greatly helped in taking the Indian message to the global platform.

She has done wardrobes for close to 35 participants in international pageants including those of Lara Dutta,

Priyanka Chopra, Diya Mirza, Diana Hayden, Celina Jaitley, Tanushree Dutta and Neha Dhupia, to name a few. She has also designed wardrobes for Sushmita Sen and Aishwarya Rai Bachchan.

All this has helped her to connect with the younger generation. In 2002, Ritu Kumar, joined by her younger son Amrish, also launched a sub-brand—Ritu Kumar, LABEL. This sub-brand uses the established forte of traditional Indian design and converts it into a fashion-oriented international product. This is aimed at the young, global Indian woman with a contemporary lifestyle.

The Other Side of Womanhood

As far as the work-life mix is concerned, Ritu's story is no different from others. Professional success also meant small compromises at home. She confesses that between work and her two sons—Ashwin and Amrish—it was purely a game of time management. "I do not think anybody has an answer to this problem. You are guilty when you are at work and you are guilty when you are home. You can neither be with nor away from your children and that is not a happy situation to be in. At one time, I could not have afforded to stay away from work but once things eased up a little, I started to spend more time with the kids. I am happy they understood and were sensitized and now at the age that I am, they have a life of there own and I have got myself a life...I look back with a great sense of satisfaction to the richness of the life that was tough but very fulfilling."

Today Ashwin is a filmmaker and a lucky one at that since his first short film, *Little Terrorist*, was nominated for an Oscar in the short film category. He is in his early 30s and has just made his full-length feature film. The younger brother has joined Ritu's business as he loves designing and has masters in business management. "We would not have scaled up business so much if Amrish had not shown interest to take it to the next level. In case he would have wanted to do something else, I would perhaps have gone back to some kind of work in the field and de-scaled the business."

Stress Busters

Ritu is a part of a fiercely competitive sector. And like every other creative field, the adrenaline is always pumping. People are throwing fits where they shouldn't be. Competition is always kicking—be it with self or with the rest of the fraternity. But Ritu has mastered the art of surviving it all.

"I go for my periodic holidays but most of the time, I fight the lows by taking a deeper plunge into my work as I enjoy it immensely. It de-stresses me. At times, I also venture out shopping and love to update my wardrobe with stuff from other designers because after a point in time, it is too dull to the eye to keep seeing only your own stuff all the time!"

But if Ritu was not a designer, she would have been a full-time painter. In her younger days, she had gone to the Fine Arts Academy and learned painting. However, as of now, there is no time even to pursue it as a hobby as Ritu is busy with using her brand appeal to attract clients to all things Indian.

"Most of the modern world seems to be severing its links with the natural and organic processes of textile production; the Indian subcontinent still retains a hold on many of its ancient clothing traditions. In its continued use of the unstitched garment, India is one of the few countries that do not follow a uniformly prescribed fashion and textile code."

Way to Go

On one hand, Ritu is globe-trotting, draping models in style to set ramps on fire. On the other hand, she is striving to keep alive the textile heritage that is buried in the undocumented corners of Indian history. Over and above this, Ritu has been making a serious effort to prevent Indian fashion industry to go the Chinese way.

"The entry of international brands has almost wiped out China's national dress and cultural identity. I do not want that to happen to India. I will make every effort to keep our heritage alive by giving it a contemporary look."

Fortunately, in her lifetime, Ritu has seen India emerge as a force to reckon with in fashion and design and Indian brands have a golden opportunity to piggy-ride the fashion industry to invade the world.

But the journey has only just begun for Ritu, who has lots of messages to weave into her collections, giving the world a sneak peek into the Indian textile tradition that must live in its fashion!

* * * * *

Competition is always kicking—be it with self or with the rest of the fraternity. But Ritu has mastered the art of surviving it all

SIX

The Corporate Alchemist

Swati A Piramal

Director—Strategic Alliances and Communications, Nicholas Piramal India Ltd

There is a child that breathes in each one of us. But rarely do we allow it to peep out and give everything that we do, the colour, spirit and energy of childhood. Swati Piramal has mastered the art of allowing the restless child in her co-habit with the seasoned adult. The child constantly keeps pushing her to the next best thing. And she moves on but not without accomplishing the task at hand with the perfection of adulthood.

As a person, Swati is somewhat of an alchemist. She loves to experiment with a bit of this and a dash of that, only to come up with a concoction as good as gold. Not a lady of routine, she is terrified of easy boredom. So she has found for herself, out-of-the-box pursuits, in areas as varied as music, management, nutrition and writing. As a Sufi mystic said: 'Let the beauty we love be in what we do'.

To her, life is both about left and right brain appeal. Her projects have a scientific sense of purpose but not without an inherent appreciation for various creative forms. Obviously, that makes the games she plays rather unconventional and interesting. She teamed up with

Mrinalini and Mallika Sarabhai to present stories of ancient science in the form of a dance opera to flag off the new Nicholas Piramal Research Centre in Mumbai.

Next, she was dabbling with Sir Edwin Arnold's work on the Gita. He wrote one of the first English translations of the Gita. Swati got together with a group of Shakespearean actors who read the beautiful verses of Arnold's poem '*The Song Celestial*'. It was then reproduced with Pandit Jasraj rendering the original verses in Sanskrit. Finally, a flamenco dancer from Spain brought the great verses to life using the dance-form. This truly multimedia and multi-cultural product was initially meant for consumption within the Piramal Group but now has found a doting audience outside as well.

Swati's love for music and science encouraged her to work on the resurrection of Rabindranath Tagore's Science Anthem that was originally written for the inauguration of the Bose Institute in Kolkata but, like many things precious, was buried in the yellowing pages of history. It was stored in a vinyl record. The team restored the scratchy sound from it and asked Javed Akhtar to do the Hindi interpretation. Nicholas Piramal finally dedicated the anthem, sung by Pandit Jasraj, to the nation.

The Piramals' love for art is mirrored in the research centre as well. A 200-feet mural by tribal artists depicts the importance of health. A huge Washi sculpture by Japanese artist Eriko Horiki lights up the lobby. Horiki is celebrated for converting the art of traditional Japanese paper-making (Washi) into an architecture and interior design element. Each lab has a piece of colourful art giving it the much-required relief and making it a great place to work.

But her quest for creativity and innovation does not stop there. As a home-maker, her kitchen is all about innovating constantly to tease the palate of both close family and buyers from foreign lands whom she hosts with finesse over red wine and sumptuous food at home. In fact, her culinary self also experimented with opening a 'back to nature' style Italian restaurant called Biscotti in Mumbai. The restaurant turned out to be something of a poetic disaster because the chef could not emotionally deal with guests putting ketchup on their pizzas and sprinkling chilly flakes on their pastas. But she went on to co-author 'Eat your way to good health', a cookbook with Tarla Dalal and a book on diet and nutrition, especially for patients with renal diseases and related disorders.

For this child of reason, who is presently heading research and development and strategic alliances for Nicholas Piramal, the cosmos is a laboratory and life is a beaker. For her, the human spirit itself was invented to innovate and improve the world and she continues to mix a bit of business, a splash of science and a lot of compassion to contribute her bit.

Through Baby-eyes

Swati was born into the Shah family in Mumbai on March 28 in 1956. She lived in a joint family with her grandparents on Marine drive in Mumbai. Her childhood was full of love and care from her uncles and aunts and her grandparents. A quiet child, she loved to hide in a corner with some books. Most of her childhood reflections center around her father's love for books and her mother's culinary prowess. Her father would take her shopping for books and let her wander about in the store or in a library for hours, looking at all sorts of books – seeing and touching the wisdom with her tiny hands. He introduced her to the best friends ever and taught her to respect wise thoughts shared by others through the written word.

In his free time with her, he would affectionately bombard and inundate her with wonderfully narrated stories from Ramayana and Mahabharata. He would narrate stories about Arjuna's brave battle against evil Duryodhana and thousands of tales that would ignite her little mind and get both her imagination and grey cells tingling. This peep into the *Bhagavad* through baby eyes during the formative years helped her build a value system that gave her the strength to stand for the just and the good as an adult.

Throughout her childhood, her father kept whispering just two thoughts into her tiny ears – be inquisitive about the world around you and gather wisdom as if there is no tomorrow. With the result, curiosity about every possible pursuit in life became a way of life for Swati. Till date, she is like a child who wants to dissect every toy that comes her way to see what makes it run.

"Every girl is influenced by this man in her life she calls dad. And I was fortunate enough to have a father who taught me that there is nothing that I cannot accomplish. He was very interested in teaching me subjects like mathematics, biology, physics, history. He would make sure, I knew all my numbers and tables. The only thing that I remember vividly about my childhood is the fact that my father never dissuaded me from knowing and discovering the world around me, especially through the written word."

This was in 1950s. Her father fed her on positivism in an era when women were only told what they could not do. They were never told that they were capable of doing whatever they wanted in life. There was a social architecture and every woman was asked and was taught to fit seamlessly into it. But her dad did not want to make Swati a cog in the social wheel. He wanted to see her as the force that gives the wheel its motion. So her childhood was bereft of mental shackles so common in that age and time.

Even though Swati's mother, an accomplished chef, taught her daughter culinary magic and shared brilliant house-keeping tips that rounded her personality as a woman, her parents never lost sight of the intellectual requirements of their daughter. Her mother took her on 'pickle journeys' where they picked unripe mangoes, sun dried chilies and made pickles for friends and family. But she also taught her that in cooking, one can see the hand of the master creator—the Lord who has given the rain and the sunshine and made available every ingredient that goes into what we eat and relish.

In short, her parents—pushing and nudging her to learn every moment of her life—spread open the world at her tiny feet and said 'Go Play'.

Formal education began with the Walsingham School in Mumbai. Her unconditional quest for knowledge and friendship with books made her a bright girl who was as serious about her math and science as she was about her debating, elocution, poetry, music and drama. For Swati, all these interests were to flower in later life when she stepped out into the world to test what she had gathered in her early years. One of her prized possessions is her school leaving certificate that says she was brilliant in voice and drama—a trait that she used with finesse in later life. The gift of Goddess Saraswati was to stay with her.

Taking from the influences of her childhood, till date, Swati's biggest expenditure is on books. She is always ready to give away a tiny fortune for a book that is older than 100 years and can spend days sifting through the pages of a book, getting their feel.

"I love the feel of old paper and I can easily transport myself into the era when the book was published—studying the kind of paper that was used, imagining how they would have printed at that time and so on. If I am fascinated with a topic, I end up reading more than 500-600 books on it and do not stop till my curiosity about the subject is satiated."

Doctor of Destiny

The quest to do medicine stuck to her very early in life when she had her first conscious brush with a professional that the world sees as a 'doctor'. One of her cousins had got a vaccination and developed a reaction. Everybody was panic-stricken. They all loved and wanted to help the suffering child but nobody could do a thing. Finally, the doctor *sahib* landed and everyone's face lit up as if they had seen Almighty Himself walk into the sick child's room. He took control of the situation and Swati's ambitious mind took control of her, telling her this was the calling she had to pursue.

She spent her pre-medical years at Xavier's College in Mumbai where she become an editor of "*The Xavierite*"—satiating her love for the written word and won laurels for the college in debating. She then went on to study medicine at King Edward Memorial Hospital in the University of Mumbai.

As her medical pursuits progressed, so did her friendship with Ajay Piramal. The two were introduced by a cousin of his, who was in school with Swati, at her birthday party. She was just 16 then. The relationship stood the test of time as the two continued to meet at social events and birthday parties. Finally, she got engaged to this man of finance who was studying business.

And it was providence that brought them together. For building a successful pharma business later, Swati's knowledge of medicine was important. But equally important was Ajay's financial acumen. Till date, that is how the duo works—him on the finance side and her on the medical side. They complement each other.

"Ajay is feminist—he really believes that the potential of Indian women can be unleashed to create a powerful new force for India. Without his active support, I could not have achieved anything. He respects my creative and scientific ideas and encourages them. When I suggested we buy the HMR Research Centre, he agreed in five minutes straight! Jokingly, he said it would be a gift for my birthday and would be better than even the most precious pearls! I learn constantly from Ajay—he is spiritually very strong and has a calm disposition."

Swati intended to complete her medics before getting into the wedlock. But Ajay's father, Late Gopikrishna Piramal wished them to marry as soon as possible. The elder Piramal was a textile millionaire who started with trading in cotton and later went on to buy the Morarjee Mills which was listed on the Bombay Stock Exchange 135 years ago.

But he seemed to be like a man in a hurry. He asked his son to take over the reigns of a company called SS Miranda when the latter was only 23, giving him absolute freedom to experiment with the business. And as if having an insight into the future, he wanted Ajay and Swati to marry at the earliest. Swati's parents thought that she should complete her medical studies and at 20, she was in no way prepared for marriage. But her father-in-law threw in an irresistible bait.

"He told me that if I married soon, he would build an entire hospital for me so that my career and aspirations did not take a hit. And I sure walked into the honey trap."

She married Ajay in 1976 and her father-in-law died suddenly in New York just four years later. Obviously, he had wished to see the kids settled before he bid farewell.

But after the death of Gopikrishna Piramal, his brother Ashok Piramal kept the promise and gave Swati the land to build the hospital. So armed with just a tiny bit of knowledge in medics and no experience whatsoever in building, running or managing even a house, she got into bringing up the Gopikrishna Piramal Memorial Hospital in Mumbai. In 1983, the charitable hospital started work, treating physically-challenged children.

After this rather reluctant but enriching stint with project management, in 1984 Swati went to the College of Physicians and Surgeons, Industrial Medicine, Bombay to hone her medical skills further.

Journey to the Awakening

Life was one cushy, satisfactory journey with everything chugging along the track—smooth and nice. But one day, as Swati was driving down to the factory in Parel that happens to be the home of cloth-mills in India, her soul took a bump. The region was endemic for polio because the mill workers were all migrants. They used to come from the villages to the city and most children they had, would have polio due to lack of immunization.

"As I was driving, I saw this four-year old girl who was completely paralyzed. She had quadriplegia where you are paralyzed in all four limbs. She was lying there watching the world pass by while other children in her vicinity were laughing, skipping and running around. I was shocked and something inside me retaliated and said that cannot be. The sight, somehow, shook me from within and I knew I had to do something."

Swati thought hard and finally got to work. She set up a rehabilitation centre with an early objective of treating children with polio in the region. She wanted to have a no-polio zone of 10 kilometres in the area because it was the worst affected and needed intervention the most.

But Swati soon realized that by beginning with cure, she had started at the wrong side of the spectrum. She had to start with the root cause and prevention. She had gone wrong in doing what any other doctor in her place would do. She started all over again by trying to convince them to get immunized. But that met with great resistance since the lot thought that polio was the result of the wrath of the Goddess and not because of disease-germs. So, her team decided to crack it in a more innovative way. They began to take the softer route to the psyche and hearts and more importantly to the mind-set of the worker families, through various art forms.

"We did street plays, skits in Marathi and we addressed them through music. They gradually opened up and mothers started bringing their children for immunization."

Then came the second challenge. They would stop at the first dose and not complete the three doses that were imperative for the eradication of the disease. With the result, the children still had polio and they were fast losing both trust and interest in the concept of vaccination.

Swati fought frustration and decided to take it a step further. She stumbled upon a brilliant idea. She went to her brother-in-law and told him she wanted 1,000 meters of cloth that he could pass off from the seconds or some stuff that could be spared from the textile mill. He obliged and Swati rolled out the incentive scheme. All mothers who would complete the dose of three vaccines for their children would get one meter of cloth as appreciation after each vaccination.

"It worked. About 25,000 children were treated every year and in a span of a few years, polio was conquered and the rehabilitation centre had to be shut down for want of patients. This infused confidence in me that one could prevent disease by using innovative methods rather than spend only on cure. Eradication of polio in that area cost me 1000 metres of cloth. If I would have had to treat the children with polio or give calipers it would have been very expensive and maybe difficult to afford for any individual trying to make a difference."

The biggest victory, however, was that she saw the four-year old girl who had stirred her conscience to begin with, walk out of the centre aided but upright.

Territories - Untried and Uncharted

The Gopikrishna Piramal Memorial Hospital had taken off and was helping physically-challenged children. For the want of managerial knowledge and a formal education in management, Swati developed her own managerial style. While on the job, she developed some interesting management insights that were soon to become the culture of the organization.

"It was the culture to give the patient a hug or a pat at the back, to pick up a child and make him feel wanted with the warmth of care. These things helped the centre to develop a culture of love and kindness that trickled down and was talked about."

But Swati was not satisfied at that. She wanted to be sure that the quality of health care meted out to the underprivileged people coming to the hospital was no less than the treatment that a millionaire would get at the top-most hospitals in the city. So, she sat down in a quality class with expert learning about the Japanese quality standards —to bring Kaizen into the working of the hospital. Nobody had applied these management practices, limited to manufacturing, to the area of health care.

There were small but rampant problems like the waiting time faced in the doctors' room by people. That meant taking a day off from work for those patients who belonged to the economically-backward strata and that really hurt and dissuaded them from coming for treatment. In short, it was loss of money. The team measured the time and used management methods to cut down the waiting time to about 10 minutes. Patients acknowledged that and appreciated it.

Later she experimented with practices related to small conveniences for patients visiting a hospital—small things that can make the harried experience of going to a hospital more livable. The hospital, for Swati, became a hotbed of experiments in management.

She did not stop even after the hospital became the first charitable hospital in India and one of the few in Asia to achieve ISO 9002 certification.

Quest for Perfection

In 1992, after giving birth to two beautiful children—Anand and Nandini—the quest to become a professional manager got the better of her. Breaking all conventions associated with Marwadi women in India, she left her kids and husband at the age of 37 in the patronage of sisters-in-law—Urvi, Gita and Devina and packed up her bags for a Masters in Public Health from Harvard.

"I had this sinking feeling that while I had a grip on medicine, I was wanting in management. My knowledge of management was acquired by hit and trial on the job. But I needed a formal regime to understand what accounting, marketing, communication and automation was all about."

She took all these questions to Harvard and got busy in finding answers. She worked with experts like Professor Walt Willet—one of USA's foremost specialists in epidemiology of chronic diseases like coronary heart disease and cancer. She specialized in marketing, corporate communication, especially related to health care. She also had the honour of being selected to speak on women and health care as the Harvard University's Commencement Speaker at the 1992 graduation ceremony.

Interestingly, her mother Arunika went with her to Boston. At 63, her mother was still learning and enrolled in the Cambridge School of Culinary Art. The fragrance of her biryani would waft through the windows and young hungry students would gather around and crave to get a spoonful of the Indian delight.

"The imprints of those days are quite visible in Nandini, who went to Oxford University and then to Stanford for her MBA. Nandini loves gourmet food and she has inherited culinary skills from her grandmother. She would often organise parties in her dorm that would be full of spicy Indian food that her friends still remember her by. For three generations down, cooking has been a relaxing pastime but unlike Nandini and me, my mother had actually enrolled for a formal culinary course at Boston."

And while they were at it, Ajay decided that he wanted to do a post-graduate programme and joined Swati in Boston. The kids followed for holidaying with the parents. It turned out to be a fun and family stint that made the sabbatical an even more memorable one. While the couple was sold over the knowledge incubation in Boston, the children still remember the fun with snow, the jugglers, and students playing the guitar on the campus.

In her success, however, a woman can never stand alone. In addition to a supportive husband, there inevitably are other women who stand like pillars. They weave a support system that a working woman can partially rest her responsibilities with. If it was not for the joint family system, Swati may have had to think twice about her stint at Harvard or staying away from her children.

"In my case, my mother was a great support. My sisters-in-law were always there, standing by my side, whenever I needed them. Living in a joint family was a blessing at that time—a blessing that only few get to partake in these days of nuclear culture. I can never thank them enough."

The Learner Returns

Having conquered her zest for management, Swati returned home to join the professional ranks of Nicholas Piramal—the company formed after Ajay Piramal acquired the Australian pharma major Nicholas Laboratories that was exiting India in 1988.

But by then, the entrepreneur in her was at full bloom. She devised and discovered divisions and products within the group that became incubation projects in themselves.

The year 1992 was also the early days of computerization and Swati had specialized in information technology; with relation to health care at Harvard. She brought this knowledge back home and into the company.

"We formed a task force to rapidly implement enterprise resource planning solutions for meeting the US

FDA standards in manufacturing. We set up a wide area network using satellite network technology to determine sales online, reduce the working capital and waste in supply chain."

And then there were many firsts within the IT infrastructure of the company. She went on to institute datawarehousing solutions and distributed resource planning to build greater efficiencies into the company's processes. The company introduced web-enabled e-business solutions. The research centre also came to gain from the knowledge of best-in-the-breed practices that Swati had acquired during her stint abroad. Those were the early days for information technology but Swati did not look for any re-confirmations on whether or not to deployment the new systems.

"All that paid off for the group as we started getting bigger business and more revenues due to greater efficiencies and a seamless back-end."

There were other projects that added value in the long run. She headed the task force to set up a national diagnostic network of pathology laboratories. The group acquired the HMR Research Centre in Mumbai and set up path labs across India to be part of a chain offering histopathology, immunological specialized tests. The concept has expanded to 35 cities now. The Wellspring Clinical Facility was founded and she started the Clinical Research Organization for the group. So within the larger framework, she kept starting new divisions, new products, and incubating newer pursuits.

Conviction—the Will to Win

In early years, trained like a scientist and guided only by logic, Swati was not much of a spiritual person. Her world was guided more by the proven word of wisdom whether it came form science or from people who surrounded her.

"When I met Mother Teresa for the first time, it changed my life. She had come to our hospital and planted a tree. But the way she touched the paralyzed children, the way she carried herself and the kindness written on her face, would inspire anyone to give his all. And she taught me that when there is a resolve to help and make this world a better place to live, God walks by your side."

After the visit to the hospital, as the group was driving her down to Vasai where hundreds of sick people were waiting for her blessings, the highway traffic became very congested. We were getting very late. "Let's pray" she said and as if guided by the divine police, the trucks seemed to move aside to let us pass. Her message was loud and clear—Nothing stands in the way of good intentions.

The other guiding axiom that Swati swears by and that probably owes its genesis to her father's influence, was that the consent to health or to illness, to happiness and to sadness, lies within each one of us.

"One can finally get only what one wills for oneself. This remained the guiding force of my life throughout my years of struggle—with self and at work. If there is passion for what one wants to do in life, the universe

The Winning Couple: With Ajay Piramal

lines up for you. Fate is important but it falls on its face if there is no deep driving desire. Life is not the caprice of fate."

Interestingly, Ajay too has lived a life guided solely by his father's value system and his own conviction. There is an interesting story of grit that goes behind his acquiring Nicholas. In 1988, Australian major Nicholas Laboratories was exiting India. Established Indian companies were stepping over each others' toes to walk away with the pharma company. Mike Barker—the man in-charge of the disinvestment had laughed at the dream of this 33 year-old, untried entrepreneur who wanted to take the company that ranked 48th in India into the top five. Barker may have laughed, but he did not brush away the conviction with which Ajay made the bid. A decade later, Nicholas Piramal was not just in the top five but went on to acquire other companies abroad. It acquired the Indian subsidiaries of F Hoffmann La Roche (Swiss), Boehringer Mannheim India (Germany), Rhone Poulence India (France), ICI from UK and the Hoechst Research Center (Germany) and also a number of acquisitions in Europe and North America. Thus is the power of conviction.

In the Classroom of Life

When Anand was seventeen, he was attending a summer school in the Italian city of Venice. Admiring the art and architecture of St Mark's Square, he told his teacher that there was nothing like that back home. His teacher corrected him gently and told him how much he respected the rich and ancient Indian culture that has shown the light to the rest of the world for thousands of years. On returning home, Anand decided he needed to understand his own culture, to begin with.

"We requested a young Swami from the Chinmaya mission Br Sattvikji to teach Anand the *Bhagavad Gita*. That's when we got involved as well and started studying it once a week. It was Anand who led us to this new insight of our ancient art and culture. The child is the father of man!"

Along with conviction, however, there were many more attributes to learn as Swati moved on in life. The more life brought her in contact with enlightened souls, the more she became like a sponge, soaking in good thoughts flowing in from all directions. She got initiated into the world of Yoga through Father Jo Pereira, who is a catholic priest but also the most wonderful teacher of Yoga and meditation. There was the spiritual head of the Hare Krishna temple—Radhanath Maharaji—in Mumbai who taught her a lot about life and the real meaning of compassion. . . She went to listen to lectures by management thinkers. For about an year, Ajay and Swati studied the Gita. The year initiated them into the realms of the metaphysics where life gets a new meaning and the game of the cosmos becomes much simpler to understand. They emerged with greater understanding of *Gyana* yoga, *Karma* yoga and *Bhakti* yoga as taught in the Gita.

For the first time, Swati started assimilating the wisdom behind the childhood stories that her father used to narrate. She understood the wise words that had stood the test of 5,000 years in time. In a world where each one of us fights the battle of life each day, confused and unassisted in our respective pursuit of truth and of justice, she found the guiding light that holds strength for those who intend to be just and good. She became a true student of the *Bhagavad Gita*.

Lessons in Management

In fact, the exposure to Gita did not just change the way she perceived life. It also added profound and deeper meaning to the principles of management. She understood benchmarks of quality, man management and corporate ethics that were set thousands of years ago by wise men from India.

Above all, she discovered what Mahatma Gandhi had said: The Gita is of immense practical value that is applicable in daily life. And the lessons kept unfolding in their lives and business with each passing day.

One Saturday morning, the two students of *Bhagavad* were bogged down at the Piramal household. There was tension in the air. The company was in trouble and the family was under threat of arrest. The culprit was Phensedyl—a simple cough syrup that the company manufactured and had been selling for 50 years. But for reasons which were patently unjust, the authorities went after the company charging it with drug trafficking and other charges under the Narcotics Act even though a cough syrup is a medicine and not a narcotic under the law. The family had no idea how to fight the situation that was created to wipe out their reputation and goodwill. They were finding it difficult to gather courage to rise and fight.

They were listening to Pandit Jasaraj's rendering of the *Bhagavad Gita* where Arjuna is told to fight for the right by Lord Krishna. The sermon that explained how Lord Krishna exhorted Arjuna "conquer your enemies and enjoy the glory of sovereignty. I have already slain all the warriors. You will only be my instrument" acted like a clarion call and the family got together to fight what was unjust. They decided to rise and conquer the enemy and within weeks the storm subsided.

But that was only the beginning. As each day unfolded the treasure tucked away in the book of the wise men, their resolve to share it with their colleagues became stronger. To share the light, Ajay and Swati went on to write the book '*The light has come to me*'.

The wise word started guiding them in everything they did. "Wise men do something and the multitude will follow"—they read and set out to introduce quality standards that would make them best-of-the-breed globally. "We started to get all our manufacturing sites up to the world class US FDA standards."

This spiritual quest for perfection reflects in their office where Swati and Ajay have created nine Zen gardens with granite sculptures reflecting important verses of the *Bhagavad Gita*. They commissioned noted sculptor Adwaita Gadnayak to make these out of pure black granite. Swati takes all her foreign visitors for a tour of the art and its cultural importance.

Taking India to the World

Being a part of an Indian MNC that sells to over 100 countries and has plants in four countries and is still growing, Swati has to travel a lot. And she uses this opportunity to share the pearls of wisdom with the world. She has strived to show the world that there is an Indian way of doing everything and it is the right way.

One day, a friend from abroad came home over lunch. While they were at it, the crows were crowing noisily outside. Interestingly, the friend told her that in her country, there was a ministry that was responsible to shoot the crows coming into the city. But in India crows are treasured for being environmental journalists—a natural resource that is to be cherished—just as any other living and crawling creature. We all remember our grandparents lifting tiny insects and putting them on the fence outside the house so that they would not get trampled upon by the movement in the house. Such is the Indian way of doing things.

And when translated into a management style, this wisdom is being recognized the world over as the most successful way of managing people and assets.

"We have people from 22 different countries working for us. It's a pleasure to introduce this multitude to the Indian way of management and certain values that people still haven't understood fully elsewhere in the world. We take some of these tenets from Gita and apply them in business and that has changed the way we work. We have learned that all are equal in the eyes of the Almighty and we respect all people and all cultures."

"And it may sound absurd but here in India, we are forced to believe that value system can flow into animals too." The Piramal family will never forget the day when Sunny, their naughty little puppy, sneaked in and tried to remove a pearl necklace from the house in the middle of the night. There was however, Magic, the older dog, who took it from the mischief monger and put it right back where it belonged.

Statements of Style

Along side good management practices, Swati worked on her personality in creating a style statement that would make people take her seriously as a well-meaning businesswoman. She started travelling on her own and getting comfortable with nearly everything but for eating alone in the evenings.

"I learned to carry myself amongst different audiences and cultures, making sure I was taken seriously and got my due as a woman professional. When I am abroad, I make it a point to wear a sari. One, it differentiates you and people notice you in a crowd. That accomplished, it's time to do some sensible and intelligent talking and you have established the right connect as a professional."

Swati, who loves all the bright colours of the world and is comfortable wearing the pinks, oranges and loves her greens and purples, consciously drapes saris to become an acceptable ambassador of the country she represents.

"I am never self-conscious of being a businesswoman and being from India. In fact, that instills a sense of

When abroad, Swati consciously drapes saris to become an acceptable ambassador of the country she represents

pride because even the west and the orient have yet to accept and appreciate women as centres of power. There is no need to ape any nation, we are an example unto ourselves and I live up to that expectation when I am carrying myself abroad."

Interestingly, Swati's curiosity does not rest even in matters of dressing. She is intrigued by the various forms of saris that India has on offer and it has come to be a favourite topic of her secret pursuits. She leaves no chance to study the motifs and various types of borders on her saris or the history of the weavers who weave them. Recently, someone sent her a Paithani sari which is over 80 years old. That became quiet an assignment because Swati wouldn't rest till she had dug out every bit of information on that sari that was to be found through friends and on the net.

Journey—the Long & Short of It

Is Swati a child of Providence? In certain but limited ways, yes. Destiny had set out a dotted line and she kept relentlessly joining the dots by grabbing each opportunity that came her way to weave a good life at home and at work.

"Upon hindsight, the fact that I got married at 20 became the greatest enabler for me to balance out the personal and professional responsibilities. With early marriage and motherhood, I had performed the most critical family responsibilities by the time my career gathered steam. In the earlier years, I had the luxury of working part time. Once the kids reached college, I started giving more time to my career."

Now that both Anand and Nandini have joined the company, she has even more time at hand and seems to be getting drawn deeper into business. Success and failure in building a healthy and a balanced family, to Swati, is also situational. There are no sure shot recipes for success or disasters in relationships.

"The biggest truth in a working woman's life is that you need patience to handle work, home, relationships, children—all simultaneously. People have to deal with the cards laid out by destiny in a graceful way. If you learn to enjoy every moment, celebrate every role that you have to play in life—be it that of a wife, mother, a friend or a co-worker, it's the entire battle won.

The message obviously is that even if you do not get what you like in life, one needs to like what one gets and enjoy every moment. If you take life as it comes, everything falls into place like a jigsaw puzzle. At least, it did for me."

The modern day woman may think she can make her family live out of cans. But she can claim victory only if she is as successful in giving her family a healthy lifestyle as she is in filing patents for the products of her company.

But as a mother and a wife, Swati certainly has not lived a life without self actualization. One day she sat with her kids and asked them if they had ever felt neglected or found her wanting in her duties. She got the most valuable feedback of her life.

"My kids tell me that I have done a good job with them. They never drink carbonated drinks and are used to only fresh juices. They thank me for teaching them to eat healthy and maintain a healthy lifestyle. They tell me that they are happy, I had been doing something constructive with my life and not spending my entire time getting into their hair."

But there certainly were some lessons that she had to learn along the way. She has learned to slow down a bit and pull the reigns on her impulsive self. She decided to do things with meticulous precision even if that means doing fewer things at a time. And she has picked up lessons on juggling relationships. In fact, she learned a neat trick on that one from another successful businesswoman, who constantly faced the problem in keeping everyone happy.

"When sometimes you can't be there, take the effort to call that person and say: Look I'm really sorry I am not there but I want you to know I am with you and thinking of you. That gives them due importance and they never forget that you remembered."

Her success in striking a balance in personal and professional life has made her believe strongly that women who help themselves can attain remarkable heights. To begin with, they need to believe in their talents, in their capacity to take any problem head on, whether it is at home or about their past or people at work. And fortunately, Indian women have this capacity. It is innate—inside of them.

Fruit of Labour

As a professional, Swati has seen her zenith and is still evolving. The Prime Minister has nominated her as a member of his Scientific Advisory Committee, on the board of Council of Scientific and Industrial Research (CSIR) and ex-President of the French Republic Jacques Chirac conferred on her the award of '*Chevalier de l'Ordre National du Meritr*' (Knight of the order of merit). Recently she was awarded the prestigious Rajiv Gandhi Award. And credits keep flowing in.

As a landmark, she remembers the day she got a letter from the American ambassador. She was invited to meet the then President of USA Bill Clinton who was arriving in India on a state visit. The invitation was to be kept a top secret and only half a dozen people who the US government thought would be the biggest influencers of generation next, were invited. The rendezvous was a small Irani restaurant. Swati met the President and ably presented the case of the Indian pharma industry. As a result, an Indo-US co-operation programme in life sciences and biotechnology was started.

"I realized along the way that in the goal of getting to the highest standard you can ask for and get help from even the most powerful people on earth."

Vanaprastha—Beyond the Known Path

They say when you are in your 50s, you come to terms with your immortal self and you start looking at other things that lie in the realm of metaphysics or philosophy.

Indian Institute of Management
Lucknow
LAKSHMIPAT SINGHANIA - IIM, L
NATIONAL LEADERSHIP AWA
23rd December 2006, The Ashok, New Delhi
In association with
MIPAT SINGHANIA
ION FOUNDA
K. Industrie

It's a call to understand what the divine is all about—the quest for the ultimate or the supreme knowledge. This has now become the greatest pursuit of the woman who has lived life king-size but now wants to get to the meaning behind the madness.

"I am presently writing a book on medieval romance. The romanticism set in the XIII-XIV century. I am completely fascinated by what I am calling—'A call to the path'. I visit bookshops all over the world and go online all the time to look for books on philosophy, to figure out if somebody knew the answers to the questions regarding the ultimate truths of life."

She is also digging deeper into the realms of all religions and schools of thought with the spade of her inquisitiveness to find answers to the unknown and unearth the lost wisdom that was set in India in the bygone centuries. She is studying assiduously the sacred literature of Buddhism, Sufism, Vedas and vedantic treatises, day in and day out, to get a feel of life in those centuries that fermented such immense knowledge.

"I go through them with the greatest regret of having lost most of the originals. They are all gone. I want to try and bring it back in a form that any Indian, wanting to go back to his roots, can relate to."

A New Beginning

Swati acknowledges the setting in of *Vanaprastha* (the phase of life where the person retreats from worldly life and lives with limited material possessions)—but it's not *Vairagya* or *Sanyas* (renunciation) that's on her mind anytime soon. Recently, she was invited to the Ranthambore game sanctuary. In the evening, the group decided to drive outside the reserve—a little further into the adjoining areas. For the first time, she visited a place where there was no electricity. It was seven in the evening and everyone was asleep because there was no light.

"India is such a big country and there are so many ways in which you can contribute that I get the feeling that this is just the beginning for me. I will never be wanting for the lack of things to do. I looked at that sleepy little village and thought to myself: This can't be. How can a part of us be lighthouses to the world and rest live in abject darkness?"

Desire Unearthed

Swati travels the world, wearing upon her the assertion that India is an idea whose time has come. "For many years, we have been infested by colonial mind-set where nobody seemed to believe that we could get there. There was a serious shortfall of self-worth. In every conceivable list, we were at the very bottom—be it quality of life, availability of a car or a phone or even the basic amenities of life - we did not figure anywhere. But times have changed and India is emerging out of the shadows of failure. To everything now, there is an Indian way of doing it right."

Macro goals apart, Swati is still bubbling with baby-like fantasies that she would love to explore at some point in time. Ajay and the kids may sometimes find it hard to keep up with Swati's enthusiasm and zest. But her positivism is her life-force. She remains an extrovert, feeling comfortable surrounded by people. She is as energetic about her next presentation as she is excited about the next party at home.

"I would like to make a film. And I would love to produce a play with an Indian theme which premiers on the Broadway. I know it is outlandish but that's what dreams are all about."

Married for over 30 years now, Ajay has quite learned to live with the child in Swati, who inevitably takes control at home. Like all wives her favourite complaint is why the family can't spend more time together. Why they can't take a short holiday? But the two have shared so many interests and pursuits in life that there is no space for dissatisfaction—neither with life nor with each other.

At work too, she spends a better part of her time dreaming of the next innovation. She yearns for an India-discovered drug to go global.

"I am confident that we will soon see the day when a drug discovered here will save lives not only within India but of millions outside. I spend most of my working time figuring out how we can do it, how will it be funded, how can we cover up the risks?

For this woman of many dreams who has lived over half a century of achievement, the world is still a playground and there are many more goals to strike and many more goal-posts to cross.

* * * * *

SEVEN

Pocket-sized Powerhouse

Vinita Bali

Managing Director, Britannia Industries

It was one of those glittering evenings that companies weave around a new brand being born. The top echelons of the corporate world were socializing and celebrating over the launch of a new product in Nigeria.

A gentleman, suave and polished in his immaculately tailored evening suit, walked up to a lady in the corner of the room to exchange pleasantries.

"So, what does your husband do?" he asked.

"I do not have one," she replied, bemused by the man's assumption that she had to be married to be here. But he was only following logic as most women at such a 'do' had to be the spouse or secretary of some very important man! He would not let it rest at that. To tide over the embarrassment, he quickly jumped on to his next assumption.

"Oh, I beg your pardon. Then you must be working," he asked presuming that she must be assisting one of the corporate top shots present at the 'do'. Again he was following the logic of the time and age when women could be trusted only with handling senior management's time and appointment diary.

"I work with Cadbury in sales and marketing," the woman replied. But he seemed to have jumped off the wrong side of the bed so he decided to stick to the topic.

"You must be working for him?" he said naming a person who was quite senior in the Cadbury hierarchy.

By now, she had started enjoying it and pat came the reply: "No, he works for me."

It was 1992 and it turned out that the gentleman had been in conversation with Vinita Bali—the Marketing and Sales Director for Cadbury Nigeria and a member of its Board of Directors.

This was not the first time, for it had become a game that Vinita had enjoyed playing many times over, in various roles and in various countries. She had bumped into similar assumptions—be it during her stint in the UK, or when she became the youngest general manager for Cadbury India as well as in Nigeria and South Africa, where she worked in different capacities for the chocolate gaint.

The world's somewhat condescending attitude towards this small-framed woman did not change even after she went on to become vice president and head of strategy for the Coca-Cola Company, reporting directly to the chairman and was one of the three division presidents that the company has ever had. But Vinita hardly allowed this to come in the way of her quest to conquer, thanks to her positive disposition. Along the way, she learned to brush aside such stereotype conventions and move on.

This Delhi girl, who now holds the mantle of Managing Director of Britannia Industries, believes that opportunities in life come as a wave that waits for none. One either surfs to conquer the wave or ducks to let it pass. If there is one brave reality about her life, it's the fact that she seldom allowed an opportunity to pass by even if it seemed distant and unsettling. Her biggest strength till date is her love for adventure—be it in sport or life.

"Perhaps there is something called destiny but we shape it by the choices we make and what we do with situations and opportunities that come our way."

Toddler Steps

In childhood, Vinita was something of an antithesis of her present self. Born on 11 November 1955, she was a stubborn kid who wanted to be left alone. If something got into her tiny little head, it had to be done and it had to be done without delay and quite the way she wanted it. And she was happiest and best when she was left alone, inventing games, playing them and making merry in a world of her own creation. In a nutshell, she did not hold much promise as a social creature.

"I liked to be by myself or at best with adults—my parents and an aunt who lived with us."

To mend her daughter's reclusive behaviour, her mother Amrit, who had a refined taste for the arts and music, enrolled her into Kala Vihar—a school of dance, music and painting run by the renowned Manjushree Chatterjee—a disciple of the legendary Shambhu Maharaj. But her daughter sat in a corner for weeks, just watching other kids, showing no sign or desire to interact with other *Homo sapiens* her size.

"I kept to myself, though I would spend every evening at Kala Vihar. But something must have been taking shape within, for finally, to my mother's delight, I came back home one day and proclaimed that Kathak was worth giving a try."

Her parents were delighted to see their daughter break out of her shell to begin what would be a lifetime of eclectic interests, lots of travel and friends from around the world.

Vinita remembers her parents as her soul mates. They were two different people temperamentally—with her mother being a great storyteller who enjoyed books, music, meeting people and poetry and father Kundan, being more inclined towards academics and the pursuit of knowledge. So they contributed in complementary ways to her growth and development. One of three kids, Vinita has two younger brothers—and all three remain close and connected even though they have not lived in the same city or country for almost three decades now.

"Right through, my parents were very supportive. Dad was always keen that we did well in studies. But, he equally respected our extra-curricular activities. Even though he was not musically inclined, he made it a point to attend all my Kathak performances and encouraged me in what I was doing."

In fact, Vinita's journey from childhood fantasies to reality was a rather amusing one. As a kid she wanted to be a bus conductor as she was fascinated by the man who stood at the steps of the bus collecting all the money and distributing tickets.

"I thought he was the one who was in absolute control of who boarded the bus, where it went and when it had to stop. A little later, I was hooked to the idea of flying planes and soaring in the sky. Then I switched to the dream of becoming a neurosurgeon as the parents of a close friend were both doctors and looked very busy and impressive all the time. These fantasies lasted till I was 11 or so."

Life, however, had different plans chalked out for her and the tides of destiny took her to several shores around the world but not as a pilot or a neurosurgeon!

The Dance and the Discipline

She remained a serious student of Kathak and devoted 12 years to the dance form as a disciplined student—five days a week. At one point, after her first 'solo' performance when she was 15, she even started thinking that Kathak was good enough to pursue as a career!

Vinita's love for the classical dance form gradually branched out, initially thriving on the fact that, for the first time, it had given her a platform to make friends, learn about music and the arts and look beyond herself.

The rigorous and regular Kathak practice gave her personality a sense of purpose and joy

Later, as she grew up, the love blossomed because she started respecting the discipline that it had inculcated in her. The rigorous and regular practice gave her personality a sense of purpose and joy.

"I learnt a lot besides dance from Kathak...and I have the greatest admiration for my guru—for her discipline, for the hours of practice every day and her patience as a teacher. I was also extremely fortunate to meet and interact with great artists like Maharaj *ji* himself (Shambhu Maharaj), Nikhil Banerjee, Girija Devi, Latif Ahmad Khan, etc. The singular passion they all shared was the pursuit of perfection. That left an indelible mark on me—the fact that you practiced long and hard every day, no matter how good you already were."

The Achievers' Spark

In addition to being a student of Kathak, Vinita was an all-rounder at the Convent of Jesus and Mary School (CJM), Delhi and participated in almost everything—from sports to dramatics. In hockey, she played center-forward and in gymnastics her hand-stand was outstanding! She recalls her dramatics training in school with great enthusiasm as she had a chance to work with people like Sushma Seth, Barry John and Zarine Chaudhury.

Vinita was class captain right through and became the head-girl of CJM, a trait that stayed with her, for she went on to becoming the vice president and later president of the Lady Shri Ram College students' union. And both in school and college she won awards for "outstanding qualities of leadership".

Hand of Providence

It was the summer of 1975 and Vinita had just got admission in Delhi School of Economics and Jawaharlal Nehru University to pursue Masters in Economics after completing her graduation at Lady Shri Ram College. She had also secured admission to IIM Calcutta as well as Jamnalal Bajaj Institute of Management Studies at

Though Vinita does not have enough time for pets, she loves theatre and particularly enjoys language films

Bombay University. But Masters in business was the last thing on her priority list as her chosen pursuit was to complete a Masters in Economics, sit for the Indian Administrative Services exam and opt for the Indian Foreign Service.

However, that was not to be. Her cousin who landed up at their place to spend a few days in Delhi, became the ambassador of change in her life. He persuaded her parents to send their daughter to Mumbai to study business for the exposure she would get from staying away from home. He also convinced Vinita that she could write the IAS exam even after her management degree.

"So theoretically, I left Delhi and with it, the thought of a masters in economics not because I was yearning to study management but to experiment with Mumbai. For the first time, I was going to live in a hostel."

Little did she know that she left Delhi at 18 only to travel far and wide. After that first step, she went on to live and work in six different countries and five continents, and travelled extensively to 45 countries around the world.

With her leaving Delhi, lots of things changed. She became a student of management, started staying on her own for the first time and owned up Mumbai. But certain things remained a constant. While at Jamnalal Bajaj, she continued to pursue her love for theatre by participating and winning prizes at Mood Indigo, in addition to staging a play for the public titled 'Next Time I will Sing to You', directed by a batch mate.

Business Basics

Professional success was to begin with the first initiative she handled as a management trainee with the Consumer Products Division of Voltas in Mumbai. The most remarkable achievement from those days is the launch of the Rasna Soft Drink concentrate—a drink that added great vitality to her professional life.

Vinita got lucky as she had great professionals to hand-hold her at her first job. Rasna soft drink concentrate was a novel proposition and India lapped it up. And in the process, Vinita learned the ropes of brand management from the best-of-the-breed.

"I greatly respect Usha Bhandarkar who was the Creative Director at O&M at that time and Roda Mehta who was the Media Director. Even though I was a young trainee, they were extremely patient and invested a lot of time and effort in guiding me. I was fortunate that at the start of my career, I got to work with the best people both within and outside the company."

After two-and-a-half years of rigorous training in brand management, Vinita got an opening with Cadbury India as Brand Manager for the entire chocolate confectionery portfolio, which was repositioned by Vinita, based on path-breaking research insights. The result—sales doubled in three years.

Her favourite lines from Robert Frost aptly describe the way she has approached life—'*Two roads diverged in the woods and I chose the one less travelled by…and that has made all the difference*'

Destiny Came Calling Again

The next opportunity came veiled in a joke that Vinita was cracking with a friend over the phone. She was on a call with an old friend who had won a Rotary Scholarship to study in the US. As they were talking, her friend suggested that Vinita apply for the same scholarship. Vinita was reluctant as the last date for filling the forms was only a day away. But her friend insisted and got her a form that Vinita filled on the fly.

"We went into a scramble, filled the form and managed to submit it within the deadline. To my surprise, I got an interview call and before I knew it, I had earned the graduate intern scholarship of the Rotary International that basically covers all your expenses for an year."

So Vinita had a one-year fully-paid scholarship from the Rotary International to pursue higher studies anywhere in the world. The only catch was that she did not have a university to go to as she had not applied to any. So once again she went into overdrive mode as the last date for admissions to universities abroad was just a few weeks away and she had yet to appear for her

In school, Vinita participated in almost everything—from sports to dramatics

GMAT! She got ready for that, simultaneously applied to postgraduate courses in several universities and finally went to Michigan State University at East Lansing. So, as if pushed by the hand of providence once more, she packed her bags for postgraduate studies in Business and Economics at Michigan State University on a scholarship from the Rotary International Foundation.

Vinita had been Cadbury's first woman executive and had proven her worth for the company by then. Therefore, Cadbury was happy to grant her study leave, post which she could come back to the company. Vinita wasn't sure for she thought she may be attracted to stay back in the US for a Doctorate. But she accepted the offer and was to inform Cadbury during the course of the year if she decided to stay back in the US to pursue a PhD.

Learning from Everywhere

Being a student in the US was rejuvenating. There was a lot to discover and unlike India, the syllabus and courses were not regimented or time-bound. And there were some surprise packages that made the stint even more memorable. She was selected from the University for the Graduate Internship Program at the United Nations.

"We were a group of about 60 students from all over the world. There was a common agenda where we would attend the Security Council or the General Assembly deliberations during the morning and work on our respective projects in the afternoon. As an intern, it was a heady feeling to work out of an office in 1, UN Plaza.

The cafeteria was most interesting as you got to meet people from over 140 countries. On hindsight, it was the same as the Coca-Cola Company in Atlanta in terms of the diversity of people from different countries."

Vinita got to work with the Centre for Transnational Corporations which was part of the UNDP. She worked on reports and research topics like the role of telecommunication in South East Asia and the role of MNCs in economic development. These reports were finally to make their way into the UN library.

"The other high point of this internship was that we were eligible for tickets to Broadway shows for 90 cents. So all the interns really had a blast and made the most of this perquisite."

For Vinita, those years were golden and couldn't have been better—living in New York and discovering its myriad delights. Next, she was one of the two students selected by the university to participate in the Global Leadership Program in Washington. The topic for the summit was energy sources and conservation.

"There were 20 of us from about 15 countries, who went to Washington, stayed with different families and got the opportunity to meet and interact with congressmen and senators as part of this leadership program. We also attended some congressional briefings and had to present papers on energy sources in our respective countries. The exposure was overwhelming and I understood, for the first time, the energy sector and the politics surrounding the subject."

In the mean time, she had also finished her 45 credits and was planning to move to New York or Columbia University for her Doctorate. But soon, she decided that a Doctorate in management was very boring especially as she did not see herself in full time academics.

"I had a great time going back to school but academic management did not really excite me. So I informed Cadbury that I wasn't pursuing a Doctorate after all. They offered me a job in England. I packed my bags and landed in Bournville where the confectionery business was based."

With lady luck on her side, she stayed for two years in the quaint town of Bournville, by the Bourne brook where John Cadbury had invented eating chocolate. She was the Group Brand Manager and part of the team that launched one of the most successful new products of the time—Wispa, which was an aerated chocolate.

"I was again in a new environment and earning in pounds for the first time, Europe was so accessible and I started Europe-trotting big time. This also enabled me to stay connected with several European friends that I had got to know as a student in the US."

An Eye-witness to History

Vinita came back to India in 1986 to head marketing and rose to become the youngest General Manager in Cadbury India. In 1991 and as part of a young leaders exchange programme, Cadbury offered to send her to Nigeria. The idea was to send her there as sales and marketing director and on the board of Cadbury Nigeria, and get the head of sales and marketing in Nigeria to come and work here to know the Indian market, in readiness for bigger responsibilities thereafter for both.

The assignment was valuable but not without some surprises and unforeseen challenges. When she went there in January 1992, the official exchange rate was nine naira to a dollar and during March of that year, the currency plunged to 23 naira to a dollar due to a massive devaluation. It was a herculean challenge to grow the market.

Vinita feels: "If you have a sense of purpose and passion, in many ways, what you end up doing becomes a process of self selection"

"In those unprecedented and most difficult conditions, we grew the business and made money for the company. I worked for an excellent MD, Dr Christopher Kolade, and learnt a lot from him not just about business but about leadership and humanity."

Before she could return to India, Cadbury offered her yet another challenge. Given the turnaround in the business in Nigeria, they saw an opportunity in South Africa to transform marketing and sales in the context of hopes and aspirations of the new South Africa. This was towards the end of 1992 and South Africa was bracing for elections in 1994 with the talks between the African National Congress and the National Party in full swing. The offer given by Cadbury was: If Vinita thought she hadn't had enough action already, she could head straight for the country.

"I was somewhat apprehensive. Being neither white nor black, I did not quite see how and where I would fit in the social fabric of the country."

So they struck a deal. Vinita would go and travel the country, meet people, look around and then take a call on whether she wanted to move there or not.

These were the most interesting times for South Africa. Nelson Mandela had been released in 1990—hope and optimism were pervasive. The more she travelled around and met people, the more she wanted to be in that country.

"I got this strong feeling that I wanted to be a part of the history of this country and working for Cadbury South Africa would give me that opportunity. So I decided to go to South Africa in 1993 instead of coming back to India."

Destiny had chosen her to head the marketing function in South Africa in 1993-94 at a time when the country was undergoing its most profound transition.

"I still remember walking and driving around on the day South Africans voted in April 1994. It was such a moving experience; I learnt a lot about grace and patience from that one experience. The euphoria was palpable and ubiquitous."

As things were advancing politically, so were they culturally and socially. In fact, with the black population going mainstream, there was a whole new way to understand and connect with people as consumers.

Under the able stewardship of Vinita, Cadbury South Africa reinvented its marketing, transformed its brands and made innovation center stage in all aspects of marketing and sales. Here was Vinita's chance to test and try all the axioms which she had learned in her years of marketing and sales and develop new strategies for a unique marketplace.

"We realized that we knew very little about the majority of consumers—their preference for categories and brands, what they consumed, where they bought, why they bought and how they bought. So it was an expedition of learning and discovery…I worked with some fabulous people."

The first time Vinita said she wanted to do a market visit in Soweto—the largest black township near Johannesburg—people thought she had lost it. Who went for marketing calls to Soweto? But for Vinita, that was the only way to learn. She had to go and see it for herself rather than imagine what that market was like.

So Vinita's life became a voyage of discovery—living in different countries, adapting to different cultures, witnessing the making of history, closely.

"The biggest thing I learned by living in different countries was culture. The next thing I learned was flexibility, adaptability and the importance of being non-judgmental. All of these experiences played a role in shaping me up as a person."

Coca-Cola Calleth

After a long innings with the chocolate major (Vinita thought she would retire from Cadbury—she was having such a good time), another opportunity came out of the blue. The Coca-Cola Company, under the stewardship of the marketing genius Sergio Zyman, was scouting the globe for marketing talent. They tracked Vinita in Johannesburg, flew her to London to meet Sergio and others. In less than 48 hours after the interview, Vinita was offered the role of the Worldwide Marketing Director for Coca-Cola, based at the corporate headquarters in Atlanta. So in August of 1994, Vinita headed to Atlanta from Johannesburg. She was responsible for the worldwide strategy for brand 'Coca-Cola', the most valuable brand in the world. For a marketing professional, this was a dream come true!

Vinita was out to do her best again as she worked with the team to double the historical growth rate of the brand. And she had her timing right too. Atlanta was getting ready for the Olympic games of 1996 and Coca-Cola had been a sponsor of the Olympics since 1928. Now the games were in its home town.

"Coca-Cola was a key sponsor and I was the worldwide marketing director of the brand. What else could I have asked for as a professional? The experience was intense and gratifying."

A large part of Vinita's success and the sharp focus on the brand globally, came from path-breaking work she lead in understanding the core essence and iconography of the brand and translating it into strategy and initiatives that made the cash register ring incessantly.

In 1997, she took over as Vice President of Marketing for Latin America, and in 1999 relocated to Santiago in Chile as President of the Andean Division with consumer sales in excess of $1 billion. She was responsible for the company's business in Chile, Ecuador, Bolivia and Peru. With a progress report like that there was no dearth of recognition.

In 2001, she was made a Corporate Officer and appointed Vice President and Head of Strategy, reporting to the Chairman. In this role, she also created a 'think tank' for the company covering subjects as diverse as the environment and innovation processes. After two years of doing this she was restless. The company was going through its own transition.

"I joined when the company was at its peak—the combination of Roberto Guizetta as Chairman and CEO, Doug Ivester as COO and Sergio Zyman as CMO was unique. We were ready to conquer the world and we did. By 2003, things had changed a great deal… Coke began to lose some of its edge."

Meanwhile, her mentor at Coke and the globally acclaimed marketing guru, Sergio Zyman had left the company in 1998 and created a highly successful consulting practice in Atlanta. Sergio had persuaded Vinita to join his firm and in July 2003, she made the transition to consulting. She became the Managing Principal and Head of the Business Strategy practice at the company's Atlanta office. As a member of the Board of Managers, Vinita shared responsibility for developing and managing Zyman Group's consulting business which doubled that year.

"Again, it was a desire to explore new horizons and work with Sergio that made me leave Coke and join the Zyman Group."

That in a way, completed the circle of her being a transformational leader who started her voyage to discover Nigeria and landed at Atlanta via Johannesburg and later, Santiago.

Mammoth Muhammad: Her well-being comes from the diversity of exposure that she has had and the opportunity to meet so many different and wonderful people

Vinita was still in Atlanta on her consulting assignment when her mother came down with a paralytic stroke. That forced her to rethink her priorities and she came to the conclusion that she wanted to be close to her parents as they were getting older, especially with her mother's illness.

"I had left home when I was 18 and reckoned it was time to be back with my parents. I decided to come back to India even before I knew what I was going to do."

Three years ago, Vinita came back to India and joined the Nusli Wadia-managed Britannia Industries Ltd as the Chief Executive Officer. Within a year, she was promoted to the position of Managing Director. She is also on its Board of Directors.

At Britannia, she spends most of her time accelerating the growth trajectory, energizing innovation and bringing about a business and cultural transformation.

We the Women

Being a woman in the corporate world and that too from a developing country like India, especially in the 80s, always tagged a novelty to Vinita wherever she went.

"People are initially intrigued ...but that lasts for a short while. Once they interact with you and see you at work, they very quickly accept you for who you are—as a professional and as a human being."

The trick for women is to see themselves and be seen as professionals and not go around with a chip on their shoulder, expecting to be treated differently. The attitude and demeanour with which they conduct themselves has a lot to do with how women are accepted at work or elsewhere.

"You cannot go around with the 'I-know-it-all' arrogance. You do not have to be seen as the coolest or the smartest one around. Just being yourself...being authentic... goes a long way."

In fact, as Vinita worked with different organizations and in different countries, she formed a hypothesis around why women usually excel in their professional pursuits and often out-perform their male peers in most organizations globally. Being a woman and in many cases the first one to join a large professional company, she has experimented with the various facets of being a minority in the male-dominated world of business.

"Women can and do change the political landscape of an organization. Being a minority, the desire to excel is high and so is the consciousness to accomplish a task well. As they shine in their work, they create a performance and effectiveness ceiling for their male peers instead of hitting a glass ceiling themselves."

Once you start contributing and delivering results, a mature organization stops noticing gender. Gender actually becomes irrelevant and competency takes over.

"You have to make gender irrelevant so that peers are not thinking of you as a man or a woman but as a competent resource. You have to get them to a point where they respect and value you, your talent and the results you bring to the table."

And that can happen only if there is ability and competence together with belief and confidence in oneself.

"My first credo is not to be afraid to explore. If you have a sense of where you want to go and are keen on getting there, do not let gender or anything else stand in the way. Trust that things will fall into place and go with the flow.

Sometimes I look back and think, if I hadn't explored the opportunity of going to Nigeria, would the rest have happened the way it did? Very difficult to say because one thing led to another—Nigeria led to South Africa, which led to Coca-Cola in Atlanta and then Chile."

If one were to look at Vinita's book of professional axioms, it has three questions that she has used as career litmus all along. Every time she made a move, she asked herself three questions that made the decision easy.

"I always asked myself: 'Is what I am doing meaningful for the company. Is it something that I will learn from and will I have fun doing it?' And if the answer to all the three is yes, I choose to stay with it. Otherwise it's time to move on."

Living Life on her Terms

Outside work, Vinita has several interests that she actively pursues. She has kept her interest in music and dance alive 'largely through listening and interacting with people who are passionate and involved'. Her musical repertoire includes western and Indian classical music—vocal and instrumental, *ghazals* and old film songs. She loves theatre, films and shares her interests with several friends, both in India and abroad. Having stayed across the globe, she particularly enjoys language films.

"I have friends in Atlanta who always call any film that has sub-titles a 'Vinita-kind-of-film.'"

She loves to travel as well and has made the most of combining her work-related travel with discovering lots of new places. "I travelled almost 150 days a year, for several years when I was with Coke and made it a point to discover something about each country I travelled to."

On being single, her response is matter of fact. "It isn't as if I sat down and decided that I was not going to

Vinita loves to travel and has made the most of combining her work-related travel with discovering lots of new places

marry or that there were no guys around. The one thing I was clear on was that I was not going to get married because it was mandatory or the conventional thing to do. I have followed my conviction on most things and gone with the flow…"

But, at the core of it all, Vinita is a person who is very independent and lives life on her own terms. Her favourite lines from Robert Frost aptly describe the way she has approached life—'*Two roads diverged in the woods and I chose the one less travelled by…and that has made all the difference.*'

And her conviction says if she were to live her life all over again, she would not change a thing, "...except for seriously learning how to swim as a kid…I could not master my breathing in water!"

Dress Not to Kill

As a non-executive director on the board of Titan Industries Ltd, she is teased for being the worst customer that Tanishq has ever had. Vinita, who is seldom seen wearing jewellery, is a marketing challenge for the folks in the jewellery business. Talk about diamonds or pearls, if you like, but you will never catch the gleam in this woman's eyes.

Interestingly, Vinita stands out as a woman professional who derives her confidence from the mettle inside and not from the dress she dons or jewels she has on her. For her, the biggest asset is her multi-faceted exposure to various cultures and the multiple dimensions of her personality. "My well-being comes from the diversity of exposure that I have had and the opportunity to meet so many different and wonderful people, while exploring new lands. I can handle a business talk and salsa with equal ease. That is my style."

She hates to paint her nails and allows a manicure and a pedicure, provided they promise to finish it while she is having a hair cut. She keeps her hair short so she does not have to blow it dry. Her idea of fashion is what she feels good in….and the range goes from business suits when she is travelling abroad, to saris, *churidars*, *salwar-kameez* and blue jeans for the weekend! You will never spot her tip-toeing on high heels. She would rather dress smartly than be fussy about the whole affair.

Interestingly, unlike her peers, she spends her money shopping for old maps, engravings, etchings, pottery and carpets. And of course, books.

Future Perfect

"I do not think I will ever retire…as in not do anything with life. Right now, I enjoy doing what I do. If somebody had asked me fifteen years ago where my life was headed, I do not think I would have been able to guess even half of what I have done so far. So, these things are best left to be discovered."

But there is one thing that Vinita is sure about. If you have a general sense of purpose and passion, in many ways, what you end up doing becomes a process of self selection. To borrow one of her favourite lines from Faiz Ahmed Faiz, "*Faiz thi raah sar-b-sar manzil, Hum jahan pahunche kamyaab aaye,* (Faiz, the journey was in itself the destination as I arrived accomplished and successful, in all pursuits of life)."

*****

EIGHT

The Grit behind the Glamour

Vandana Luthra

Founder, VLCC

The story of Vandana Luthra is a tale of two different Indias. It is representative of the conflict between convention that has tied the Indian woman in shackles, and conviction that has made her break through and stand for her rights.

In fact, it has a heady blend of the reel life converging with the real life spiced up with all the excitement of a Bollywood blockbuster. The first half shows Vandana as the pampered daughter, growing up in a posh mansion of 'a silverware-served, upper middle class, Oxford-read family with a stiff upper lip'. But the second half has her as the daughter-in-law, struggling to break ice with a family where education and career are considered a male bastion.

Vandana spent a larger part of her productive years working towards gaining the affection and respect of her husband's family where the ultimate dharma for a woman was to keep a home and a husband and everything that comes with it. Her story has the glamour of this chic, thoroughly pampered damsel crossing the chasm between the shining India and the part of India that suffered for a long time, not due to poverty or lack of resources, but purely due to lack of imagination.

And all this for love—for the commitment of spending her life with the man who she met at a Christmas party when she was 16 and fell in love with. As a woman born in independent India and coming from a fairly modern background, she was not bound to make the effort to win them over, but she allowed her career and aspirations to take a backseat till she had earned the love of her in-laws.

Her marriage to Mukesh Luthra was like bringing together the same poles of two magnets. While Mukesh and Vandana were made for each other, there was a seemingly insurmountable incompatibility between the cultures of the two families that were coming together in marriage. Both families lived at two ends of the cultural spectrum.

Bridging that educational and cultural divide has given Vandana's life a sense of fulfillment. She certainly deserves a cheer for building a beauty empire of over 135 centres across more than 65 cities in India and overseas, from a very humble beginning. Today she employs nearly 6,000 people and Vandana Luthra Curls and Curves that has come to be popularly known as VLCC, is expected to clock a turnover of Rs 1,000 crore in the next couple of years.

But more deservingly, she stands as a role model for the average Indian woman for not allowing her marriage to suffer due to lack of maturity and tolerance.

"If I had not married Mukesh and lived with his family, I would always have missed the warmth and the learning that the relationship and the family brought to my somewhat plastic and superficial lifestyle. It did seem like mission impossible in the beginning. But on hindsight, I realize that the lessons in human relationship that I learned with them, gave me the emotional maturity to employ and retain thousands of people, especially women, who were to carry the VLCC brand forward in my years of business."

There is one obvious truth about womanhood that most people miss out on. A woman who can manage a household successfully can run an entire business flawlessly. The challenge and vagaries of raising a family and keeping a hearth can prepare a woman for taking the world head on. Managing a family successfully is the best learning ground and quite akin to managing a business.

And about her line of business, Vandana has a firm belief. "Being healthy and presentable is most essential for self-esteem. I have seen lives transform with people having fought acute illnesses and psychological barriers by shaping their outer appearance. For me, the way you look has a lot to do with complimenting your inner confidence."

Blessed Baby

Vandana was born to be pampered and spoiled with over solicitous attention as the first daughter in a joint family full of sons. She had come as a breath of fresh air and therefore, came with the license to kill. As a child, she could bend any rule. Interestingly, her mischievous self was a matter of delight in the family where her only brother was expected to demonstrate a regimented and disciplined behaviour.

"As a child, I always remember myself as being somewhat out of control. I was thoroughly pampered and could get away with murder, and even at that age, I was fully aware of my limitless powers. So there was no stopping me."

Vandana was born on 12 July 1959 to doting parents. Her father, Ram Arora, was a mechanical engineer and started his career with German major Siemens and stayed with them for the next forty years of his life. And for

Baby Vandana with brother Nishit, Ram and Kamini Arora: Being the first daughter in a joint family full of sons, she was born with a license to kill

him, Kamini, his wife was the most beautiful woman who walked the planet. He adored her and took the initiative to get her educated so that she feels comfortable in a family where three generations had gone to study abroad. All the women in the family were educated, so he took it upon himself to facilitate formal education for Kamini.

"If there ever was a man obsessed with his wife, it was my father. He tutored her and she was no less than a baby to him. As we grew, I would hate going to movies with them with friends around because they would watch the movie holding each others hand. As a child, I felt my ears burn with embarrassment, but they did not care less."

When Vandana was 13, her father realized that the indiscipline that had been tolerated so far could ruin her life, so he cracked the whip, though gently. Even though, by then he had risen to the position of being a Director at Siemens and had a Mercedes parked in his portico, he started making Vandana ride the local buses. He wanted to gradually initiate his dreamy-eyed daughter into the realities of life so that she could appreciate the comforts that she had been blessed with.

Little did he realize that to his spirited daughter this harsh measure was no more than an adventure. She loved it all. She did not mind walking to the bus stop or riding the bus to school or later to college.

"I was such a happy and carefree person. Everything that happened in my life was one big adventure."

Tell-tale Signs

It was summertime and Vandana was travelling to Nainital, where the family owned a cottage, to spend her vacation. One morning, her mother caught her giving the *chowkidar*'s kid a royal haircut. But that did not come as a surprise to her as she had noticed the style streak in her daughter and realized that Vandana could not keep her hands off fashion. She had sat through a reasonable number of facials and massages given by her daughter to all and sundry, to recognize her child's pent-up talent.

Vandana would spend hours styling, cutting and sewing dresses for her dolls and later went on to decide the cuts for her own dresses as well. When her mother saw this, she bought her a sewing machine and Vandana became her own dress designer.

"I was the kind of a child who would wear trinkets, jump atop the dining table and start dancing. I would look at a dance sequence once and copy it, step by step at home." Her mother enrolled her in Bharatanatyam classes to channelize her love for dance.

But as Vandana grew, her father strongly disapproved of the behaviour that he thought was unbecoming of a lady. He found his daughter lacking in seriousness about life especially vis-à-vis her brother who studied at St Columbus and was always top of his batch. Her father intervened to give his daughter, who was an average student, an academic direction. Vandana started concentrating on school. But she could never match her brother who went on to top his class at the St Stephen's College and later got into the prestigious Indian Institute of Management, Ahmedabad (IIM-A). He got a job with Lintas when he was just 21.

Meanwhile, under her father's able supervision and academic guidance, Vandana tided over school with a first division and joined Lady Shri Ram College for her graduation. But she did not let go of her panache for styling and beauty. So after college hours, she attended a vocational polytechnic to undertake a two-year course in beauty culture.

Santa's Gift

On her 16th Christmas, Vandana remembers being dressed in a black-and-red check long skirt and red suede boots that were a gift straight from London. She was attending the celebration at a friend's place in Delhi.

"Christmas was a big celebration for me as I had come to believe that Jesus Christ was my God since my father was a staunch *Arya Samaji* (follower of the Hindu reform movement that unequivocally condemns practices like idolatry, iconolatry and priest-craft on the grounds that all these lack Vedic sanctions). He would not allow any idols or pictures of Gods into the house. Since the only physical manifestation of God for me was the idol of Christ at school, I had owned Him up as my God. Obviously, Christmas was all important."

It was amidst these celebrations that she met Mukesh, who was a friend's brother. They got enough opportunity to know and understand each other.

"My parents were very cool and I had no reason to hide my relationship with Mukesh from them. I had confided in them and they respected it. I have yet to see another family that was so open and transparent, especially in that age and time."

Mukesh started visiting the family and my parents got friendly and appreciated the nice guy who was dating their daughter. Their love got the right reasons to flourish. And what started for the two at sweet sixteen still remains as sweet.

Control Therapy

Vandana was sixteen but she had not stopped being restless. Her parents realized that they needed to give her nervous energy a vent. At any given opportunity, when Vandana had free time, her mother would pack her off for short-term beauty courses abroad to keep her fruitfully occupied in something that interested her as well. That gave her latent energy a constructive outlet.

It was under these experimental trips that Vandana got an opportunity to visit Germany where Siemens were headquartered. Initially, she accompanied her father on business trips and later she travelled on her own.

She pursued education in nutrition and cosmetology from Germany. Subsequently, she did a series of specialized courses and modules in beauty care, fitness, food and nutrition and skin care from London, Munich and Paris.

"It was in Germany that I met Professor Jorgen Huchel and his wife who were friends of my father and were running a health centre there. The husband-wife

Standing Tall: With Mukesh Luthra

duo was a great combination with one being a nutritionist and the other cosmetologist. They greatly influenced my ideas and helped me to form an opinion on the business of beauty and wellness."

She returned to Germany many times to train under the couple. She also accompanied them to Paris where they would go for workshops on the latest trends in cosmetology and nutrition. She picked up new anti-aging treatments, studied about pigmentation, and learned how to use skin surfacing laser at the time when people in India had never heard of the concept. In fact, even cosmetologists back home were not allowed to use those machines as one was required to study dermatology before using them.

Vandana had made up her mind about what she wanted to do in life. But her father was not in a position to finance her venture as it required a sizable investment to set up a health centre. Moreover, her father did not put much store by the beauty and wellness business and was not really inclined towards his daughter getting into it.

Mukesh, however, understood her sadness and proposed that they get married and maybe that would give her enough independence to go ahead with what she wanted to do.

Her marriage was a turning point. Life catapulted her straight from a very English, non-vegetarian and modern Indian family into a strictly vegetarian 'caught-in-a-time-warp' kind of a family where time had stopped a long time ago for the womenfolk.

"When our parents met for the first time, my mother came back and coaxed me to change my mind. My father kept saying the boy is good but how are you going to survive the family culture? But, I was decided and my mind was made, so I insisted. My father said: 'I give your marriage less than two years', but my mother feared worse giving us just two months."

Finally, one evening, Vandana's father gave in to the whim of his lovelorn daughter with the statutory warning that she was to return home as soon as she regretted her decision. That evening her father sat with a glass of Chivas Regal, her mother with scotch in coke and Vandana with a glass of wine. That drink was to last her a long time for after marrying into a teetotaler family, she did not touch wine for the next 20 years.

The Cultural Nightmare

With this, started the sojourn of an educated daughter-in-law in a household dominated by a mother-in-law who had never gone to school, assisted by her sister, who was staying with them. From the north pole, Vandana landed straight onto the equator of life.

The two ladies had a hold on the house and did not want intrusion, and worse, they had nothing else to look forward to in life but the kitchen and the limited household chores. So they clung to their little possession, holding on to it with their teeth, denying the girl who had stepped straight out of a fashion tabloid into their private space.

How different were the two lives? Vandana cannot forget the morning and more importantly, her innocence, when she stepped out of the bedroom in a beautifully flowing Christian Dior lingerie and walked straight to rest her head in her mother-in-law's lap, who was sitting with others in an outer room.

"The lady was awestruck and turned to my father-in-law to get some semblance of sanity in the situation. He stepped to our rescue and asked me to go and dress properly."

None of the two sides were at fault. It was the difference of upbringing and the cultural divide that made their respective lives look unbelievable to each other.

Vandana had walked into a household where morning tea meant having your shower, getting dressed, going to the temple and then drinking a concoction of masala in milk. She missed her silverware, her Earl Greys and yearned for her battery of attendants.

"But that was it. I told myself, I have chosen this for myself and I better know how to handle it."

The girl who would not step out of bed before the clock chimed 10 and the servant walked in with her cup of tea, started waking up at 5 am along with the other ladies in the house. She started making her own tea, doing her own laundry and helping with the household chores.

Mukesh, who loved her, could not see her pitiable condition and tried to coax her to get some domestic help from her maiden home to aid her. But Vandana had enough maturity to visualize that it would be politically incorrect to do so. If she would do that, it would never allow her to become a part of her in-law's household for which she was trying rather hard.

She quietly started observing the routine of the people in the house and silently started coming mainstream. In the typical Indian household, she acted assistant by chopping vegetables and quietly observing the culinary tricks of her mother-in-law. The family had kept two dogs. To begin with, she was given the job of making *rotis* for them, knowing fully well that the two could neither show their approval nor disapproval for her culinary talent.

Every time Vandana would go home to her mother, the latter would feel her daughter's rough hands and her heart would bleed for her baby. But by then, the spirit of adventure had got the better of Vandana. She had started enjoying what she was learning in the process.

In a way, the learning was balancing out parts that had remained untouched in her early years of shielded life at her parents' house. She wanted to excel as a homemaker and that was her only answer to the dissatisfaction that she felt her in-laws were showing towards her.

After a reasonable amount of practice, came the day of reckoning. In the absence of the other ladies of the house, she got a chance to lay the table for her father-in-law during lunch. She won his heart that seemed to be much more malleable than the other members of the family. They became friends and as days passed by, he started to see in Vandana, the daughter that the family had never actually had and had missed all along.

With time, Vandana realized that the family had all the resources but there was a famine of exposure. Mukesh was very discreet with his parents and had joined work by then. He had been a loner and had never mingled with them or spent too much time with them. So Vandana decided to expose them to the 'fun and frolic' side of life. Her father-in-law took her out shopping and the first thing they bought together was a television and a Video Cassette Recorder (VCR).

This was followed by movie watching sessions that assisted in bringing the rest of the family together. They would watch old classics and while they were at it, would order eateries that the family had never ever enjoyed before. Mukesh's parents, for the first time, started seeing logic in living a full life spiced up with enjoyment and they started loving their daughter-in-law for introducing them to this amazing world of fun and enjoyment.

In the process of bringing out the adult in her, they joined her by becoming children themselves and seeing life through her eyes. The only member who had still not got around to accepting Vandana was Mukesh's aunt. She resorted to silly tricks to bring her down.

One day, when Vandana was packing Mukesh's lunch for the day, the aunt sneaked in and put an insect in the food. Vandana caught the aunt in the act and confided in her father-in-law. There was mischief in the air and Vandana loved nothing more than one good opportunity to act naughty again. Together the two drove the aunt to paranoia by planting a lizard in her wardrobe.

Those few years marked the beginning of a deep association between Vandana and Mukesh's parents. The cross-influence came into play where her parents-in-law took pleasure in the side of life that Vandana initiated them into. She, meanwhile, had started enjoying the customs and rituals that were a part of the family for generations.

Coming from an *Arya Samaji* background, Vandana found the religious influences in the house a novel change and enriching. She was eager to learn and eventually she got a temple made in the house compound where the strict norms of *praan pratishtha* (invocation of Gods or inviting the invisible Supreme soul to manifest through the idol) were followed and even today, she has *pujaris* on the roll to perform puja twice a day.

The certification in later life came from the much-relished fact that people would take Vandana to be the daughter and Mukesh the son-in-law of the family whenever the family went out together.

Vandana had married in 1980. Their first daughter Mira was born in 1981 and the second daughter Pallavi followed four years later, that is, in 1985. Mira's birth managed to strengthen the bond between her in-laws and Vandana. The grandparents were obsessed with their granddaughter and wanted to spend the entire day with her.

Eight years after their marriage, Mukesh decided to move out of the joint family and reach for his dream of building a house of his own. Moreover, his younger brother got married and the house was not big enough to support three families. They built a house right in front of the ancestral home.

Roaring to Work

Once the girls grew to a manageable age and Vandana was left with some space to herself, she decided to pick up the strings of her lost aspirations to get into business.

In 1989, Vandana set up her first beauty and slimming services centre. At a time, when few in India had heard of transformation centres, she dreamt of building India's first domain providing holistic wellness as a service—marrying scientific research and traditional therapies. That marked the humble beginning for VLCC.

"To convince my father-in-law was difficult. He could not understand why the daughter-in-law of the house wanted to take up what he perceived to be a 'barber's job'. He wanted me to do anything but this. Unfortunately, I was trained and inclined only to be in the beauty business. There was nothing else I could do. So I kept at it."

Vandana started small and was assisted by three girls while she took care of most of her clients personally. The model was unique. "Call it my innocence or the fact that I am made like that, I learned to share my profits from day one. So the girls, who were working with me, were more partners than employees. They were motivated as they got a percentage of the work that we did together. In fact, the team that I started with is still with me and all of them are now senior trainers with the company."

As she grew, she faced criticism from contemporaries because the model she was following did not seem to be sustainable. While still operating on a small scale, she kept ploughing her profits back into the business and expanding like there was no tomorrow. And very early on, she started on a brand building exercise by placing her ads in most of the premier newspapers across India.

Even though she found enough time to ramp up the business, the timing still did not seem to be perfect. In the next few years, Vandana suffered the trauma of losing three of the most important people in her life. First she lost her mother-in-law, who left her in-charge of the family and also her father-in-law who had had a stroke and had been bed-ridden for a long time.

Two months after her mother-in-law expired, Vandana was on her way to Mumbai on the invitation of Simi Garewal as her guest for the chat show called 'Rendezvous with Simi Garewal. "I got a call from home saying that my father-in-law was slipping and he was asking only for me. I took the next flight back home and Simi had all the reason to be upset with me."

Soon thereafter, her father passed away leaving a big void in her life. Until her life was an extension of her parents or in-laws, she patiently attended to those responsibilities. With three of them gone, the primary focus of her life suddenly shifted. Then there was no looking back. Vandana branched out as an aggressive businesswoman.

She did not have the benefit of any management degrees, so she followed her intuition in putting into place best practices, work flow and human resource policies.

With over 70 per cent of VLCC staff being women, working hours, facilities, and other policies had to be geared towards providing all a secure and progressive work environment, especially when India was still uncomfortable with the concept of women working, especially on any shop floor.

"I had a strange way of operating and keeping my flock together. Till the time we brought in professional managers to handle most of the lateral functions, each of my employees had my cell number and could call me any time of the day. In fact, a fair number of them still do!"

Her accessibility became an asset as it infused great confidence into those who were her brand ambassadors and were actually directly interacting with her clients.

"Even today, Mukesh sometime gets irritated by employees or clients calling me at odd hours to share their problems or lodge a feedback about the service at a particular VLCC centre."

But for Vandana, nothing can beat first-hand feedback while running a company.

Today, the VLCC family is a melting pot of diverse cultural, economic, social and educational backgrounds. The company has provided respectable means for women not only to earn a livelihood but also rolled out recognized training modules for women to become self-reliant beauty, fitness and health experts.

Adding a Dash of Professionalism

At the start of the new millennium, India had become more open to the thought of beauty, fashion and more importantly, to wellness. With time, Mukesh also realized the potential of the line of business that Vandana had chosen to be in. He joined her in 2000 to take the business to the next level. The Indian health and wellness market is estimated at about Rs 40,000 crore and is growing at nearly 15 per cent, year-on-year, according to industry estimates. But it needed a more structured approach to make brand VLCC tap a larger chunk of this burgeoning market space.

"I had divided priorities, especially with the girls growing up. I needed help to keep the show running. If Mukesh had not joined in, I would not have been able to scale it up so fast."

With the help from Mukesh and more time for ideation, Vandana mooted the idea of bringing in a foreign investor.

In 2004, VLCC received $10 million from a fund managed by the Hong Kong-based CLSA Private Equity in return for an undisclosed stake.

In January 2007, the company closed the second round of private equity funding with Indivision—a private equity fund sponsored by Future Group in which Goldman Sachs, Louis Vuitton and Citigroup are some of the major investors—investing US $10 million in VLCC at an unconfirmed valuation of US $100 million.

In parallel, the company started strengthening its cadre by recruiting domain experts across functions.

In this streamlining and restructuring, there were certainly some rumblings as the employee base that had been so used to dealing with the warm and personal Vandana, had to now deal with a professional cadre of managers whose business was to keep organizational objectives above individual objectives.

But an organized approach and professionalism did wonders for the brand that has since become the umbrella brand for various sub-brands including VLCC Health Care Ltd, VLCC Personal Care, VLCC Workout Factory, VLCC Spa, VLCC Institute, VLCC Alive Retail, VLCC Beauty Zone and VLCC Foundation.

The company has also taken global wings. VLCC has now forayed into international markets by opening seven centres in the United Arab Emirates. The second phase of expansion, to be completed by 2008-end, will take the brand to an additional five countries and a total of 28 centres in the Middle East, including Oman, Bahrain, Kuwait, Qatar, and Saudi Arabia. The company also plans to go public in 2009.

Path to the Future

Vandana has given 19 years of her life to building the brand VLCC. Now it's time to step aside and leave the operational concepts to professional managers. She has

The warmth of Vandana's personality and the jingle in her laughter is a replenished and unending resource

taken charge of the technical and training aspects, and is busy rolling new concepts and running pilots.

"Now I want to enjoy what I do more than anything. I would rather look at the organization as an outsider now and see how I can borrow best practices from others who are successful in the service industry."

She also has unfulfilled aspirations that will keep her busy for times to come. Vandana had wanted to go to Harvard after her marriage but Mukesh was young and boyish and did not want her to be more qualified than him at that time. Of course, now he does not mind her going. So Vandana wants to take a shot at higher education at Harvard.

But beyond learning and her business, Vandana is still a baby at heart. Just before her younger daughter got married, it was usual to find Vandana joining the fun with 20 to 30 youngsters at her place until the wee hours of morning.

Beyond This, Life's to Share

As one grows, Vandana feels that a fair amount of detachment sets in as far as materialistic pursuits are concerned, especially for a person who has sailed through the best and the worst of life. She has always believed that the real power of money is the power to give it away, and with time, this belief seems to have become stronger. She is inspired by JRD Tata's philosophy who said, "If you make lots of money, you must give it back to society as you have received so much love from it." Vandana has actively pursued her passion for sharing, by setting up and supporting the VLCC Foundation, which has served society for long and continues to help people by reshaping their lives.

She shares a special passion for the cause of eradicating obesity and educating the public at large about the scourge that it is. She works closely with the medical profession, through various initiatives, to educate target audiences about prevention of obesity. Her contribution has many faces in organizations like Tamanna, Amar Jyoti Charitable Trust, or HelpAge India. Vandana is also the Chief Patron of Khushii—an NGO that has been founded by former cricketer Kapil Dev. Khushii has set up a beauty and care institute at Neemrana village in an effort to empower young women by giving vocational training and equipping them for gainful employment.

For Vandana, the warmth of her personality and the jingle in her laughter is a replenished and unending resource. She spends it all and yet it all remains with her. Probably, that is the secret of beauty bottled up within her that one can partake only by recognizing the glow of her inner self!

* * * * *

